future HOPE

A Jewish Christian Look
at the End of the World

future HOPE

A Jewish Christian Look
at the End of the World

by David Brickner

Purple Pomegranate Productions
San Francisco, CA

DISCLAIMER

Most views expressed in this book enjoy wide acceptance by followers of Jesus throughout the world. However, some of the subject matter enters areas where honest differences of opinion exist even among believers in Jesus. As to those details, this book expresses the views of the author and not necessarily those of the Jews for Jesus organization.

Cover design and chart illustrations by Paige Saunders
© Copyright 1999, Purple Pomegranate Productions

Reprint Permissions
Purple Pomegranate Productions
60 Haight Street, San Francisco, CA 94102

02 01 00 99 10 9 8 7 6 5 4 3 2
Brickner, David 1958–
Future Hope/by David Brickner—1st ed., Second printing
Library of Congress Cataloging–Publication Data
Future Hope
        p.   cm.
ISBN: 1-881022-41-2 (pbk.)
1. Jewish Christians—Prophetic Outlook.   2. Prophetic Overview for the non-believer
                                                                    CIP

CONTENTS

APPENDIXES

FOREWORD

by Lon Solomon

The other day I was having Chinese food with my family. After dinner, I was amazed to see how much interest was sparked by everyone's fortune cookies. Now we all knew that there was no spiritual reality to the predictions found inside. But everyone hovered over their "fortunes" anyway. They read them to one another aloud. They laughed at them. They discussed their implications.

Maybe your experience with fortune cookies has been similar. We're all intrigued with predictions about our future, even if they're not true.

When we turn to the Bible, however, we find an altogether different situation. We find predictions about the future that are true. God presents himself in the Bible as the one who "makes known from ancient times things that are yet to come" (Isaiah 46:10).

Many of the Bible's predictions have already come true in the course of human history. For example, over 30 such predictions relating to the life of Jesus here on Earth were fulfilled with uncanny accuracy. However, there is still a host of predictions that relate to the end of the age which are moving towards fulfillment.

This is what *Future Hope* by David Brickner is all about. It's about future events that God reveals to us in the Bible. It's about future events that will lead to the end of this world as we presently know it. But it's not about despair—it's about how we can have hope as we look into the face of these impending events.

David Brickner is the executive director of Jews for Jesus. His vision, and that of Jews for Jesus, is a big one: to make the Messiahship of Jesus an unavoidable issue to our Jewish people worldwide. David believes that our Jewish people need to focus on issues like, "Where do I go after this life? Is there any reason to hope for anything better in the future? What answers does Jesus bring to the table on these issues?" And David believes that it's appropriate for Jewish people to personally investigate the claims of Jesus whether or not the rabbis say it is acceptable to do so.

David Brickner knows whereof he speaks. He himself is a fifth generation Jewish believer in Jesus. He serves as the leader of the most effective agency in the world when it comes to helping Jewish people consider the Messiahship of Jesus. David knows his Bible well and he knows how to effectively communicate biblical truth in ways that you don't have to be religious to understand.

In this book, David has grabbed hold of a hot topic. He has explained the Bible's teachings in a way that challenges Jewish people and Gentiles alike to consider the claims of Jesus as they apply to our personal lives. He has pointed us to the place where we can find hope in spite of the tumultuous events that lie ahead for us and our world.

As a believer in Jesus, I find this book comforting as well as intriguing. As a Jew, I find this book required reading. No matter who you are, I can assure you that you will find it hard to put down—even if you already know the ending.

Lon Solomon
Pastor, McLean Bible Church
April, 1999

PREFACE

I want people to know that the God of Israel exists, and that he cares passionately about this world. Bible prophecy contains some of the most startling and convincing evidence to support the belief that he does. Unlike many of today's doomsday prognosticators, the Jewish prophets penned a message of hope and promise for the future. The Bible contains that prophetic message, but many people think it is necessary to be a scholar to understand the prophecies therein.

Future Hope is for the curious, the seeker, the novice, or even the skeptic who just might be willing to sit and consider what the Bible teaches about the future, and particularly about the end of the world as we know it.

For many people, the only thing that seems certain about the future is the *un*certainty of it all. Others cannot see beyond the pain and suffering. We cannot blind ourselves to real problems the human race faces, but there truly is hope for a joy and peace-filled future. I want people to be able to discover that hope for themselves, and thought maybe a book like this could help.

Each chapter deals with specific predictions the Bible makes about the end of the world. The subjects are arranged sequentially, but each chapter is also designed to be read on its own, in any order. As you scan the table of contents, you may want to begin with the topic that is of most interest or concern to you.

Garrett Smith and I spent many hours preparing a series of

lectures that we gave together at the Jews for Jesus headquarters in San Francisco. I distilled those lectures into 11 chapters plus the appendixes you will find in this book. Ruth Rosen, my trusty editor for many years, worked hard to pound my work into the most readable form. While this book is by no means an exhaustive study of end times prophecy, it will enable you to access basic information about matters that do affect your destiny. I hope that as you read it you will gain a profound and unshakable hope in the One who holds your future.

David Brickner

David Brickner, executive director
Jews for Jesus

ACKNOWLEDGMENTS

This book is as much the work of Garrett Smith and Ruth Rosen as it is mine. Garrett did much of the research with me, and despite some differences of opinion (or maybe because of them), we enjoyed team teaching the lectures that served as a basis for this book. Ruth Rosen edited the manuscript with assistance from Debbie Wagner and Vicki Dunton. Thanks also goes to Susan Perlman for her input, to Michelle Brown and Paige Saunders for their work on the charts, layout and art, and to that special group of staff from Jews for Jesus who faithfully attended our lecture series and helped to sharpen our ideas with their questions and comments. The highest thanks goes to our Messiah Y'shua for being our Future Hope. —D.B.

CHAPTER ONE

PICKING UP THE PACE

Are we in the end times?

"'For I know the thoughts that I think toward you,' says the Lord, 'thoughts of peace and not of evil, to give you a future and a hope'" (Jeremiah 29:11).

Since time began, people have been craning their necks, trying to get a glimpse of the future. In ancient days kings had diviners, prophets and soothsayers—people who would read the entrails of animals to discern coming events—professionals whose job it was to predict the future.

People are still longing for a good look into the future. Some dabble with Ouija boards, others glance at their horoscopes in the daily paper. Some pay by the minute for phone consults with psychic readers. Others look into esoteric practices like Kabbalah and Bible codes to learn about future events. Then there are people who follow self-proclaimed gurus and channelers like Nostradamus, Edgar Cayce and J.Z. Knight ("Ramtha") who claim to see beyond tomorrow. It's natural for us to want to know what lies ahead.

Some people play with predictions for fun, but for most, the hunger to know the future is a craving for some kind of security, some kind of control over one's own destiny.

THE Y2K PROBLEM

As we approach a new millennium, there is an ever increasing fervor to know what tomorrow will bring. What are we to believe about the future? Frightening predictions of a worldwide economic collapse regularly surface in newspapers and journals. Leaders and experts in numerous fields are issuing grave warnings:

- ". . . there are 'catastrophic problems' in every GM plant." (Ralph J. Szgenda, Chief Information Officer General Motors, *Fortune,* April 27, 1998)

- "If we don't fix (the computers), there will be 90 million people 21 months from now who won't get refunds. The whole financial system of the United States will come to a halt." (Charles Rossotti, Internal Revenue Commissioner *USA Today,* April 2, 1998)

- "Some people with technological expertise think the whole 'millennium bug' issue is overblown. Don't you believe it," said Kelley. "Comments that doubt the seriousness of the problem are dead wrong," he said. (Edward Kelly, Federal Reserve Board member, *The Miami Herald,* March 1, 1998)

- "The Year 2000 problem, in my view, is a very serious threat to the U.S. economy. Currently, I believe there's a 70% chance of a worldwide recession, which could last at least 12 months, starting in January 2000, and even late 1999." (Ed Yardeni, chief economist at Deutsche Bank Securities, New York, and named *The Wall Street Journal*'s top economic forecaster of 1997)

Countless thousands are reacting to warnings such as these by storing up food and other survival supplies. Some are even planning to hole up in remote areas to ride out what they see as the coming storm. Many are gripped by terrible fears and are buying weapons to protect their families and ward off the riots and looting that they see as inevitable at the dawn of the new century.

Others dismiss "all of this end of the world talk" as just so much religious fanaticism. They are skeptical of what they see as fearmongering.

CAN WE REALLY KNOW?

Can we really know who is right? Is there a way to avoid the hype yet still be ready to face the future? Is there a balance between overreacting to and underestimating the problems ahead? I believe there is.

Time and time again, the Bible has proven to be an accurate record of past events, as well as an amazing predictor of the future. This may seem ironic in light of the fact that the Bible expressly prohibited such activities as soothsaying, "fortune-telling," witchcraft—none were to be tolerated according to the Torah. (Deuteronomy 18:10-12 is one of many passages prohibiting such things.) So it might seem to some that God wants us to stumble around blindfolded, with no idea of what is in front of us.

In fact, the opposite is true! God simply does not want people throwing themselves at the mercy of those who would profit by the desperation some feel over future events. God also knows that the dark powers people use to divine the future are deceptive. He wants us to know certain things about the future, but he wants us to know them accurately. That's why he tells us:

"Remember the former things of old, for I am God, and there is no other; I am God, and there is none like Me, declaring *the end from the beginning, and from ancient*

*times things that are not yet done, saying, 'My counsel
shall stand, and I will do all My pleasure'"* (Isaiah 46:9,10;
emphasis supplied).

God is not interested in concealing, but in making known
those future things which are vital to our well-being. How
does God's way of telling the future differ from that of a
psychic or a fortune teller? God doesn't charge anything for
that which he reveals, nor does he offer prophecy as some
type of "early edition" or opportunity to change the future just
by knowing it. God does not give us the illusion of being able
to control what is to come, but he gives us the very real
opportunity of coping with it. Many people despair over a
multitude of scenarios that seem to spell hopelessness for the
future. God has provided us with scenarios of what actually
will happen so that, rather than despair, we can prepare for
what lies ahead.

Are we in the last days? The Bible outlines three areas which
indicate that we are. The first area called "birth pangs" is a
group of events. The second area involves the state of Israel,
and the third area has to do with Jews who believe in Jesus.
Each of these categories points to a period of time the Bible
terms "the last days." For some, the end of the world is
frightening. The purpose of this book is to help you understand
what the Bible says about these things so that, rather than fear,
you can be filled with hope.

THE BIRTH PANGS OF MESSIAH

And Jesus answered and said to them, "See to it that no
one misleads you. For many will come in My name,
saying, 'I am the Christ,' and will mislead many. And you
will be hearing of wars and rumors of wars; see that you
are not frightened, for those things must take place, but
that is not yet the end. For nation will rise against
nation, and kingdom against kingdom, and in various
places there will be famines and earthquakes. But all

these things are merely the beginning of birth pangs"
(Matthew 24:4-8, NASB).

Y'shua (the Jewish way to say Jesus) gave that speech to
answer a question someone had asked regarding the end of
the world. His graphic image—birth pangs—actually
describes the times we are living in. Birth pangs (a poetic way
to describe contractions), are the body's way of letting a
woman know how close she is to giving birth. They become
more and more painful and plentiful as the time for giving
birth approaches. I remember when my wife Patti was about
to give birth to our first child. Her contractions began on the
day before Yom Kippur, 1988. That night when I returned
from the Kol Nidrei service, we lay in bed counting the
contractions. The more frequent they became and the more
intense, the closer we came to the birth of our baby. Finally,
at about 5 A.M. the contractions were so intense, so close
together that we knew it was time to go to the hospital. At
10:30 that morning, our son Isaac was born.

So it is with the birth pangs of Messiah. Jesus gave us a list
of symptoms to watch for. The greater the frequency and
intensity of these symptoms, the closer we are to the end: wars
and rumors of wars, nation rising against nation and kingdom
against kingdom, famines and earthquakes in various places. All
these "contractions" create a climate of anticipation. Could it be
that Jesus' words have a ring of reality to them? Certainly, we
know that the things he mentioned are becoming more
frequent and more intense.

"And nation will rise up against nation . . ." Look at the
nations. Many westerners thought that when the Soviet Union
collapsed there would finally be peace, that the end of the cold
war would mark the beginning of a safe and secure world. But
what has happened instead? An incredible rash of ethnic
conflicts has broken out. Whether it is Bosnia or Kosovo,
animosity and mistrust still exist and are finding ever-increasing
outlets. People who were once neighbors are warring against

each other.

When African nations escaped their colonial oppressors, they too expected that finally they would know peace and freedom. What has happened? Just take a look at the horrific price Rwanda has paid in its internal war: "In the central African nation of Rwanda, nearly a million people were killed in a 1994 fury of genocide that lasted barely three months. At the height of the slaughter Hutus were killing Tutsis at the rate of 400 an hour." (Jensen, Holger. "Genocide Flourishing as World Shuts Its Eyes" *Inside Denver*.)

There are tragic stories to tell on almost every continent. Suffice it to say that the intensity of war is definitely increasing.

"And there will be famines, pestilences, and earthquakes in various places." There have always been natural disasters such as earthquakes, but look at the trend today: in 1940, there were 51 earthquakes measuring above 6.0 on the Richter scale. In the '80s, there were over a thousand such quakes. In the 1990s there have been over 1500 earthquakes measuring over 6.0 on the Richter scale.

Despite all the miracles of modern technology, thousands of people are still starving to death every single day. For example, "Up to 800,000 may have died each year for the past two to three years in famine-stricken North Korea due to malnutrition and related diseases, a South Korean think tank said Wednesday." (March 3, 1999; *Reuters Limited*.) Some famines are due to crop failure, others are the result of war and still others are caused by natural disasters.

The Bible speaks of a growing sense of lawlessness as another birth pang: "But know this, that in the last days perilous times will come: for men will be lovers of themselves, lovers of money, boasters, proud, blasphemers, disobedient to parents, unthankful, unholy, unloving, unforgiving, slanderers, without self-control, brutal, despisers of good, traitors, headstrong, haughty, lovers of pleasure rather than lovers of God. . . " (2 Timothy 3:1–4).

Who can look at news reports without seeing an increase in lawlessness? Kids shoot one another and walk away, so callous they don't even realize they have done something wrong. An article titled, "Schoolyard Shootings" recounts some chilling incidents:

> In March, in the small rural town of Jonesboro, Arkansas, four children and a teacher were shot dead, allegedly by two boys, aged 11 and 13. The boys dressed up in camouflage, helped themselves to a small arsenal of firepower from one of the boys' grandfather's collection, and hit the fire alarm at the school. As children and teachers filed out, they opened fire, killing four of their classmates and a teacher who died shielding another child.
>
> In April, in Edinboro, Pennsylvania, a student shot a teacher dead and wounded three others at a graduation dance. The 14-year-old earlier had talked about wanting to kill people. Edinboro is a small community near Pittsburgh, a town to which many residents had moved to get away from city violence. (*Illinois School Board Journal*, May/June 1998: Article 2.)

Even the most optimistic among us can't help but see that there is a sickness in our society, and that the prognosis is not good.

Religious persecution is also intensifying. Fear grips the villagers of Sudan as raiding parties of Muslims pillage and burn the homes of Christians, raping women and enslaving children. An Orthodox Jew bursts into a mosque in Hebron and guns down scores of Muslim worshipers. Hamas "freedom fighters" kill Israeli shoppers in a busy Jerusalem market. Christians and Muslims murder one another in Indonesia. A mob of angry Hindus sets fire to a van in India, burning an Australian missionary and his two young sons alive.

People are fighting over religion today because they think they have the corner on truth and need to set others straight. Others are simply deceived by people claiming to be the Messiah, and they blindly follow those false prophets who profess to have some special insight from God. Jim Jones, David Koresh, and the Japanese cult leader Shoko Asahara all have led their followers down a path to destruction. Remember, an increase in false messiahs was also predicted as part of the birth pangs Y'shua spoke of in Matthew 24.

In speaking of these painful portents, Y'shua said, "See to it that you are not frightened for these things must take place, and it is not yet the end." He wanted people to be alert and aware, not fearful. The predictions of all these birth pangs are God's way of helping those who trust him prepare for what lies ahead. God wants people to have hope in him. Despite all the problems and pain we see around us, we can know that there is a way through it all. We can know that God is in control.

MORE EVIDENCE: A MODERN MIRACLE

And they will fall by the edge of the sword, and be led away captive into all nations. And Jerusalem will be trampled by Gentiles until the times of the Gentiles are fulfilled (Luke 21:24).

That prophecy concerns Israel and Jerusalem. Not so long ago, people tended to interpret the Bible's future predictions as symbolic. It was inconceivable to them that the end times events depicted in Scripture could possibly occur in any literal sense. All of that has changed with three recent events. The rise of the Zionist movement in the late 19th century, the founding of the modern State of Israel in 1948 and Israel's recapture of Jerusalem in 1967 have cleared the way for all the end times events the Bible speaks of to take place. The fact that the Jewish people are back in the Land and once again in control of Jerusalem clearly signals that these are indeed the end times.

The period of time that the Bible refers to as "the times of the Gentiles" began with the destruction of the Temple and of all Jerusalem. Jesus predicted this ghastly event and Titus and the Roman soldiers brought it to its terrible and complete fulfillment in A.D. 70.

Jesus' words have echoed down through the centuries. Jerusalem has been "trodden down" by the nations (Gentiles). Non-Jews have been in control of the city ever since . . . until now. With the rise of the Zionist movement, the distant hope of the Jewish people's return to the Land of Israel became a matter of pressing concern. Waves of immigrants began making their way back from far away lands.

Finally, in 1948 Israel became a state. The Jewish people were back in the Land God gave to them. This had not been the case for 2000 years! But the ancient city of Jerusalem was still "trodden down of the Gentiles." It was under Jordanian rule, not Jewish sovereignty. Then in 1967, as a result of the Six Day War, Israel recaptured the ancient city of King David. For the first time in 2000 years the holy city of Jerusalem is no longer "trodden down" by non-Jewish nations. It is now under Jewish sovereignty. Do you see the significance of this? What was inconceivable before is now quite possible. Most of the end times events that you will read about in this book could never have occurred during the past 2000 years. Now they can.

And how has all this come about? Many have lauded the superiority of the Israeli fighting force. Others have pointed to their brilliant military strategists. But when you look at the odds that Israel faced, it hardly seems humanly possible that she prevailed against so many enemies. As one historian described the situation in the Jewish quarter of Jerusalem in December of 1948: "Here lived about 1,700 Jews, including only 150 fighters, surrounded by more than 20,000 Arabs who were determined to destroy this potential stepping stone to the Jewish conquest of the entire Old City."

And of course, the odds against Israel in the Six Day War were astronomical. The British Institute for Strategic Studies estimated that Israel had about 60,000 regulars in her army, and 204,000 reservists. For weapons, she had some 800 tanks, and about 350 planes. The combined forces of Egypt, Syria and

Jordan added up to about 951,190 regular soldiers, 205,000 reservists, 1,932 tanks, and more than 1,162 planes.

Indeed, Israel's survival is a modern miracle and another sign that we are in the last days.

JEWS FOR JESUS—ANOTHER SIGN OF THE TIMES

"For I say to you, you shall see Me no more till you say, 'Blessed is He who comes in the name of the Lord!'" (Matthew 23:39)

Most people know that Jesus is Jewish, that his disciples and all his early followers were Jewish as well. In fact, when the Romans destroyed the Temple, even more Jews became believers in Jesus because they remembered that he had predicted that very event. Some scholars believe that by the end of the first century, as many as one-third of all Jewish people still living in the Land of Israel were believers in Jesus. Then came persecution and scattering. From the fourth century until the 19th century, while there was certainly a small remnant of Jewish believers in Jesus they were not noticed or notable.

In the 19th century, just as the Zionist movement was on the rise and present day children of Israel began returning to the Land, once again, Jewish people began coming to faith in Jesus. Since the 1900s, that pace has increased as never before since the first century, particularly in the last three decades. Now, as we enter a new century, more Jews than ever believe in Jesus.

Why is this significant? Because of the importance of Y'shua's statement in Matthew 23 that, "You shall see Me no more till you say, 'Blessed is He who comes in the name of the LORD!'" Those were the last public words that Jesus uttered in the Temple at Jerusalem. Earlier in his speech, Jesus had been quoting from Psalm 118. This key psalm predicts the coming of the Messiah by saying, "The stone which the builders rejected has become the chief cornerstone. This was the LORD's doing; it is marvelous in our eyes" (v. 22,23). Jesus used that passage to identify himself as the Messiah who would be rejected and one day recognized by the Jewish people as the very cornerstone, the foundation of all that the Temple and Jerusalem stood for. Here we are now, two thousand years later, and a significant and growing minority of Jewish people are saying to Jesus, "Blessed are you who have come in the name of the Lord."

There are those who think that Christians are motivated to tell Jews about Jesus in order to hasten his return. One anti-missionary laughingly quips that "Jews are supposedly holding up the show" by not believing in Jesus. But Christians who tell their Jewish friends about Jesus are not attempting to fulfill prophecy any more than the Israeli soldiers who took back Jerusalem in 1967 were. The soldiers were fighting for a Jewish homeland, for freedom, and for the Land God had promised our people. The result of their efforts is an indication that we are in the end times. In the same way, Christians who press on to tell their Jewish friends about Jesus do so because they genuinely care about their friends and truly believe that those friends will find lasting peace and eternal life—the fulfillment of God's promises—through Y'shua. And that is exactly what is happening.

See for yourself what some of these present day Jewish disciples have to say about him:

"Jesus filled the void that possessions, position and power never could and never would fill. Jesus was the answer, is the answer and always will be the answer to our deepest needs and desires. He is your answer, too. Please don't reject the answer before you ask God the question that he is waiting to hear." (Dr. Jack J. Sternberg, oncologist)

"What a revelation it was to learn that Jesus was not the personal property of the Vatican. He is ours, too, a Jew of Jews! This added a whole new dimension to my Jewish identity. Being Jewish was more than using my fists to

defend my honor and the honor of my people. After all,
the Bible was about Jews and about the Jewish Messiah,
Jesus. Further, it was written by Jews and for Jews . . . and
that included me. The Scriptures said that I could be a
part of God's kingdom and that was the best news I had
ever heard." (Norman Buskin, police officer)

"When I accepted him, it was strictly because God
showed me, yes, Jesus is the expected Messiah, and that
was reason enough to believe in him. . . . The realization
that I had become a Christian never made me doubt for a
moment that I was still Jewish. . . . I was born Jewish and
I will die Jewish. My belief in the Messiah is the natural
result of my search for God and fulfillment of my
Jewishness." (Dr. Vera Schlamm, retired pediatrician,
Holocaust survivor)

Many Jews as well as Gentiles have discovered that those
who put their trust in the Messiah Jesus have nothing to fear
and everything to hope for. If you have already been sensing
that Jesus is the Messiah and you want to join the growing
number of those who are finding hope in him, you can do so
today. Turn to page 129 for a prayer to help you receive Messiah
Jesus yourself.

God has plans. He knows what the future holds, and he
invites us to know, at least in part, what is to come. As we see
the things his prophets predicted coming to pass, we have
reason to trust God and to hold on tight to his promises. That
is what future hope is all about.

CHAPTER TWO

YOU THINK YOU'VE GOT PROBLEMS?

What is the Great Tribulation?

"There will be great tribulation unequaled from the beginning of the world until now, and never to be equaled again" (Matthew 24:21).

You are walking in a crowded downtown area. The streets are teeming with shoppers and people rushing to and from work. Suddenly you find yourself face to face with a character who seems totally out of place. He is a bit unkempt, with a look of urgency in his eyes, and he's shouting loudly (to whom you can't quite figure out). That is ... until he catches your eye. You see the sign he is holding with big red letters proclaiming: "REPENT! THE END IS NEAR!" Your pace quickens as you swerve wide to the right to get around him. "What a nut," you mutter. And on you go.

Judgment. For most, it is a topic to be avoided at all costs. We have a strong aversion to being told we are wrong—much less that we must suffer consequences for it. But that is exactly why God warns of judgment—so that people can respond positively and avoid the consequences.

In ancient Israel, God sent prophets to alert the people to coming peril. Those prophets were not particularly pleasant people. While their ways may have seemed overly dramatic to some, no one could fail to hear their warnings—and yet, even after hearing them, people failed to heed those warnings. We know from history that when Israel ignored the prophets, the consequences were dire. Wars, captivity, dispersion . . . all the things the prophets predicted came to pass. That is, almost all.

TROUBLE IS COMING

Those same prophets predicted certain events that have not happened yet. They predicted a time described as a Great Tribulation, a time that will be marked by terrible worldwide trouble or "tsuris" such as this planet has never seen. Such tsuris you wouldn't wish on your worst enemy! Y'shua also spoke of this terrible time—the verse cited at the beginning of this chapter is an excerpt from a speech he gave describing this Great Tribulation. The last book of the New Testament, the book of Revelation, gives an even more comprehensive look at these future events. It describes three sets of seven judgments, each one more terrible than the last. Suffice it to say, this time period will be unparalleled in human history.

In the Hebrew Scriptures, the more common term for this tribulation period is "The Day of the Lord." We find that term 26 times throughout the Scriptures.

> Wail, for the day of the LORD is at hand! It will come as destruction from the Almighty. Therefore all hands will be limp, every man's heart will melt, and they will be afraid. Pangs and sorrows will take hold of them; they will be in pain as a woman in childbirth; they will be amazed at one another; their faces will be like flames (Isaiah 13:6-8).

Remember that according to the Jewish calendar, a day begins at sundown and progresses from darkness to daylight. It is helpful to think about The Day of the Lord in those terms because it is not only a time of judgment; it is also a time of restoration. And while The Day of the Lord certainly applies to a time of tribulation, it also offers the promise of future hope. There is truth to the axiom, "It's always darkest just before dawn." The judgment of tribulation comes in order to bring the bright light of God's Day.

WHY THE TROUBLE?

Some might wonder how a merciful God could allow anything so terrible as this tribulation to befall the earth. Why is it necessary? Can't God set things right without all of this judgment? As we ask ourselves these questions, we can take a lesson from Neville Chamberlain and his negotiations with Adolph Hitler. Chamberlain had no clue as to the evil he was dealing with in the megalomaniac from Austria, and so he looked to work things out with as little confrontation as possible. "Peace in our time" was Chamberlain's goal. Therefore, in trying to settle things peacefully, he accommodated Hitler and so allowed evil to grow and consume all of Europe. There comes a time when judgment is necessary, when forcibly removing evil is the only right option.

Think about it. If you have a sense of moral outrage when you hear about murder or rape, embezzlement, child abuse, terrorism and so on, imagine the outrage God must feel. Day after day, year after year, these evil actions go on. But there is coming a day when God will say, "No more!" If God is going to bring an end to the injustice and suffering in this world (and he promises to do so), it must come down to a terrible trial. That trial is called the Great Tribulation and it is described in the New Testament book of Revelation.

God has been pretty patient with his creation, but a day will come when righteous anger for all the wrongs committed will come pouring down on the earth. The Bible talks about three sets of judgments during the Tribulation, using the metaphors of seals, trumpets and bowls. The seals will include terrible wars, famine, earthquakes and something described as "the stars falling to the earth like fruit falling from a tree" (perhaps referring to killer asteroids).

The trumpet judgments will include an apocalyptic storm that is described as "hail and fire mingled with blood, burning up a third of the earth's trees and all green grass." Perhaps a nuclear holocaust? There is also "something like a great mountain burning with fire thrown into the sea" that will destroy a third of the living creatures in the ocean. Another heavenly body described as a star will plunge to earth contaminating a third of the world's water supply. A darkening of the sun and the air is also predicted.

The judgments known as the seven bowls will include some kind of skin disease for most of the world's population. There will be more water pollution, this time killing all marine life. Some of the plagues will be reminiscent of the plagues God poured out on Egypt: a tangible darkness, water turned to blood. No wonder this time in history is called the Great Tribulation!

DO THE MATH

We don't know exactly when this Great Tribulation is going to begin, but we do know how long it will last: seven years.

Know therefore and understand, that from the going forth of the command to restore and build Jerusalem until Messiah the Prince, there shall be seven weeks and sixty-two weeks; the street shall be built again, and the wall, even in troublesome times. And after the sixty-two weeks Messiah shall be cut off, but not for Himself; and the people of the prince who is to come shall destroy the city and the sanctuary. The end of it shall be with a flood, and till the end of the war desolations are determined. Then he shall confirm a covenant with many for one week; but in the middle of the week He shall bring an end to sacrifice and offering. And on the wing of abominations shall be one who makes desolate, even until the consummation, which is determined, is poured out on the desolate (Daniel 9:25-27).

This passage from the book of Daniel provides crucial information about the length and events of the Great Tribulation. But it takes some effort to understand Daniel's terminology. First, the number seven is significant in Jewish reckoning. Seven is the number of perfection, and perfection carries with it the connotation of completion. The number seven is used to measure periods of time. The seventh day is the Shabbat, the day of rest. The seventh year was the sabbatical year in Israel, a year when the whole Land was to have a rest, when there would be no planting and harvesting of crops. When Daniel talks about "weeks" (literally units of seven) in this passage, he is not speaking of literal weeks but of periods of time, each a period of seven years.

In this amazing prophecy, Daniel gives us important details about two major events in history, one of which is now past while the other remains in the future. Daniel's clock starts ticking, "from the going forth of the command, to restore and rebuild Jerusalem." That decree was issued by the Persian King Artaxerxes in approximately 444 B.C. From that point in history, Daniel tells us to count off "seven sevens and 62 sevens." A bit of quick calculation tells us that adds up to 69 periods of sevens, or 483 years. If we count 483 years from 444 B.C. we see that the fulfillment of Daniel's first amazing prediction was scheduled for the first century. "The anointed One will be cut off. . . . The people of the prince who is to come shall destroy the city and the sanctuary."

The term "anointed one" is a translation of the Hebrew word "mashiach" or Messiah. When Daniel tells us that the anointed one will be "cut off" he is predicting nothing less than the death of Messiah . . . in the third decade of the first century! This is exactly the time frame when Y'shua died on a Roman cross. It is perplexing to consider why so many have overlooked a prophecy with such astounding implications. One explanation offered is that the rabbis have told us not to calculate the time of Messiah's coming (Sanhedrin 97*b*).

Daniel also predicts, on the heels of that astounding statement, that both Jerusalem and its sanctuary would be destroyed. This terrible tragedy did take place in A.D. 70—not long after Jesus was cut off! (See appendix 2.)

The prophecy of Daniel, chapter nine, has not been completely fulfilled. There is more—one "seven" of the seventy still remains to be played out. But there seems to be a break in Daniel's countdown; he indicates a time lapse between the sixty-ninth seven and the final seven. "The end will come like a flood, war will continue until the end and desolations have been decreed." The past 2000 years have been a parenthesis in Daniel's prophecy and we await that final seven: "He will confirm a covenant with many for one seven, but in the middle of that seven, he will put an end to sacrifice and offering and one who causes desolation will place abominations on a wing of the temple until the end that is decreed is poured out on him" (NIV).

Someone is going to make a covenant or treaty with "the many" for one seven, i.e. seven years. It is important to know the identities of those who are party to this treaty. The context and subject matter of this prophecy clearly indicate that "the many" are the people of Israel. The one who makes the treaty with Israel is "the ruler," the very one whose people destroyed the city and sanctuary. Titus and the Romans were responsible for the first destruction; they were mortal enemies of the Jewish people. So will it be with this future ruler. His "treaty" will be one of treachery. "...He will put an end to sacrifice and offering and one who causes desolation will place abominations on a wing of the temple ..."

Three and one half years after making a treaty with Israel (that is, halfway through the seven year period), this ruler breaks his word. Obviously the Temple has been rebuilt because Daniel tells us this ruler puts an end to sacrifice and sets up some kind of abomination (a loathsome horror that would be anathema to Jewish worship) right inside the Temple in Jerusalem.   Ultimately this ruler is destroyed in a final conflagration of enormous proportion.

Who exactly is this "ruler" who makes a treaty with Israel? Why will the Temple be rebuilt in Jerusalem, and what will this final conflagration alluded to be like?   A more detailed description will be presented in later chapters.   Meanwhile there should be no doubt that there is a time of fierce judgment and wrath that lies ahead. This is The Day of the Lord, the Great Tribulation.

WHERE IS HOPE?

Another term that describes the Great Tribulation is, "the time of Jacob's trouble." "Alas! For that day is great, so that none is like it; and it is the time of Jacob's trouble, but he shall be saved out of it" (Jeremiah 30:7).

Jeremiah says there will be a time of incredible distress for Jacob (referring to his descendants, since Jacob is long gone). Notice he goes on to say, "but he will be saved out of it." Later comes a promise: "'For I am with you,' says the LORD, 'to save you; though I make a full end of all nations where I have scattered you, yet I will not make a complete end of you. But I will correct you in justice, and will not let you go altogether unpunished'" (Jeremiah 30:11).

Here is part of the hope: that through all the suffering, Israel will be refined. God will correct and chastise his people, and the result will be restoration and the relationship that God has always desired to have with Israel. There is a hope for healing and wholeness behind God's judgment; in fact that is his ultimate purpose in judging. Another purpose served by this great distress is that God is going to punish the nations; he will punish their wickedness and pour out his wrath upon evil. But once again, through the Tribulation he will also turn the nations to himself. "The LORD will be awesome to them, for He will reduce to nothing all the gods of the earth; people shall worship Him, each one from his place, indeed all the shores of the nations" (Zephaniah 2:11).

The time of terrible trouble that this world faces is God's just judgment on all the evil the human race has done. Sadly, much of it is also the logical consequence of the tremendous accumulation of our own wrong choices. The Bible points out that the result of people's rebellion against God is a spiritual deafness to his voice and a propensity to hear what we want to hear, whether or not it is true. "The prophets prophesy falsely, and the priests rule by their own power; and My people love to have it so" (Jeremiah 5:31).

But what will happen in the end? That is what the tribulation time is about. God is saying, "Here you go. You want what you've wanted, without God telling you what is right and wrong? Well, here it is. This is what life is like without God to restrain the evil. I'm not holding it back any more. I offer you the sum total of what you've been asking for." So essentially, this tribulation to come is both a judgment on global evil and a consequence of our choices.

Yet there is an up side to all of this. C. S. Lewis says, "Suffering is God's megaphone to wake a sleeping world." Sometimes it takes the hardship, the consequences of our actions to wake us up and force us to face reality. I had a graphic demonstration of this when I was in living in New York City in 1995. New York is the crossroads of civilization, the hub of world trade, the communications capital of the world. The city is a monument to human achievement, to all that we can accomplish. Yet, when we experienced a record-breaking snowstorm, the entire city shut down. No one could move in or out of this world-class city. Pipes froze, people were stranded and some died. How incredible that the lightest, fluffiest stuff that could fall from the sky totally foiled the plans of some of the most resourceful people in the world. None of our creations or contraptions could control the tons of this light, fluffy stuff that had brought New York City to a grinding halt.

Now if a snowstorm was enough to stop people in their

tracks, just imagine what the Great Tribulation will do. There will be nothing lightweight or fluffy about it! God will bring down upon the world a sense of cosmic reality whereby people will be jarred into the realization that we are not masters of the universe. Only God is. And that is the key to finding the only path to hope.

As long as human beings cling to the illusion that we are the lords of our own destiny, we will be in darkness. Our illusions may bring pleasure and they may bring temporary satisfaction, but only the truth can bring us real and lasting meaning. The truth is, God is in control. The truth is, he cares about you and would like you to accept the relationship he offers those who trust him.

The Day of the Lord begins with a terrible descent into the darkest time in human history, but its ultimate goal is a bright future. There is an old Russian proverb, "The morning is wiser than the night." There is a Bible verse that says it even better, ". . . joy comes in the morning" (Psalm 30:5b). Things look different and yes, better, in the light of day.

You don't have to wait until morning to know the reality of God's loving sovereignty. When we acknowledge God as creator and king, when we give him the proper place in our lives, when we receive the life he wants to give us in his son Y'shua, we pass from judgment into the brightness of his holy presence. You can experience his truth, love and forgiveness today, just ask him. You can use the prayer on page 129 as a help.

CHAPTER THREE

THE GREAT DISAPPEARING ACT

What is the Rapture?

"Call upon Me in the day of trouble; I will deliver you, and you shall glorify Me" (Psalm 50:15).

Is there hope for deliverance from the Great Tribulation and the terrible judgment mentioned in the last chapter? Should we just despair or take an "Eat, drink and be merry, for tomorrow we die," attitude? Is there a future hope? Absolutely. God has demonstrated over and over that whenever he pronounces judgment, he also provides a way of escape; a viable alternative to tsuris. That is God's nature—righteousness tempered by great mercy. However there is one crucial contingency that applies when it comes to deliverance from God's judgment. We need only to look at two very dramatic examples of God's judgment from the past to see what that contingency is.

GOD'S PAST DELIVERANCE
The first example is Noah and the ark. The Bible describes

25

the days of Noah as a time when the human race was rapidly expanding across the face of the earth. But, at the same time, there was a marked lack of restraint from the evil that people were doing to one another. Violence and evil were so rampant, so pervasive throughout the earth that God could no longer tolerate it.

> So the LORD said, "I will destroy man whom I have created from the face of the earth, both man and beast, creeping thing and birds of the air, for I am sorry that I have made them" (Genesis 6:7).

It is frightening to think that God's judgment could be so swift, so complete, and perhaps from our standpoint, so ruthless. Yet God had every right to be filled with holy disgust over the rank corruption mankind's evil choices wrought upon the world that he had lovingly created. It was God's right to wipe the slate clean, to purge out the cancer that was multiplying on his earth and begin fresh. But God's judgment would not fall on everyone.

Enter Noah and his family. The Bible says that Noah walked with God. He had a relationship with the Lord that didn't merely affect what he believed; it characterized the way he lived his life. Because of that relationship, God committed himself to delivering Noah and his family from the worldwide destruction that was to come. You know the story—God told Noah to build a ship large enough to house his family, animals and all the supplies they would need.

This building project must have appeared bizarre to Noah's neighbors. Perhaps they mocked and ridiculed him for building a ship in the middle of dry land. But all mocking and ridicule surely ceased when the rains came and the flood waters rose. God's judgment literally flooded the earth but he delivered Noah and his family out of that judgment. As the waters of God's wrath came down upon earth, the ark and all those in it were lifted above the flood waters and saved.

A second picture of God's judgment and deliverance is the story of Sodom and Gomorrah. Fourteen of the 66 books in the Bible use Sodom and Gomorrah as an example of judgment. God tells Abraham about his plans for judgment in a very interesting prelude to the actual event (see Genesis 18). Abraham's nephew, Lot, lives in the area that is slated for God's demolition, so like a good uncle, Abraham begins to argue with God and to bargain with him for his nephew's future. Finally, God promises Abraham that if there is a *minyan,* only ten righteous ones, in these cities, for their sake alone he will withhold judgment.

Even so, Lot and his family did not make a minyan and no one else qualified as righteous. In fact the whole town was ready to rape two messengers who appeared to be ordinary men seeking shelter in Lot's home. These messengers were actually angels sent by God to help Lot and his family escape certain destruction. They grabbed Lot and his family members by the hand and literally transported them—lifted them up and set them down outside the cities. Lot's family was removed from the place by the mercy of God. There was only one condition they had to follow: as God was raining down fire and brimstone to destroy the two cities, those who escaped the judgment were not to look back. One person in the family failed to obey that condition: Lot's wife. She met her doom the moment she looked back.

GOD'S FUTURE DELIVERANCE

The pictures of how God's judgment has worked in the past give us the insight we need to know what to expect in the future. When God brings the final judgment of tribulation on this earth, he will provide a way of escape just as he did in the past. But for whom and based on what contingency does this apply?

One doesn't have to be a hero of the Hebrew Scriptures like Noah and Abraham to escape God's wrath. If God holds true to form, he'll lift all of those who have cared to have a relationship with him out from the wrath that he is going to pour out on the world. So much for the who.

As for the contingency, it is simply this: God delivers us according to his plans; they are specific, and they are designed to show that we trust and believe him. God did not tell Noah to build a high tower, he did not tell him how to waterproof his house. He told Noah to build an ark, and he gave him all the necessary specifications. For Lot and his family, the plan was much simpler. Once they were removed from the city, all they had to do was keep walking and not look back. We believe that Y'shua, Jesus, is God's plan for all who trust him to escape judgment.

Y'shua uses the same two examples of past judgment to speak of the events surrounding his future coming and the end of the world.

> And as it was in the days of Noah, so it will be also in the days of the Son of Man. . . . but on the day that Lot went out of Sodom it rained fire and brimstone from heaven and destroyed them all. Even so will it be in the day when the Son of Man is revealed (Luke 17:26;29,30).

We need to believe God when he says judgment is coming, and we need to believe him when he offers a way of escape.

As for the rescue from the judgment that will come on this earth, there isn't too much information about it in the Bible. The information we do have leads us to believe that deliverance will come in the form of something you may have heard of: an event called the Rapture. Rapture comes from a Latin word, which is the translation of a Greek word meaning "caught up." This word conveys the idea of being seized or carried off in a sudden swoop. It happens in a very brief moment and catches people unaware. In the New Testament, when Rabbi Saul, better known as the Apostle Paul, is explaining what is in store for followers of Jesus in the future, he uses this very word to describe God's deliverance.

Then we who are alive and remain shall be caught up together with them in the clouds to meet the Lord in the air. And thus we shall always be with the Lord (1 Thessalonians 4:17).

This Rapture of God's followers will be unlike anything the world has ever experienced, and it will utterly astonish those who are left behind.   Suddenly, in a moment of great deliverance, God is going to snatch away his followers from off the earth. They will be met by Messiah, "in the air." In God's mercy, his followers will be lifted up out of the midst of the earth to escape the coming judgment. Imagine thousands upon thousands of people vanishing at the same moment, nowhere to be found. This is the great disappearing act of all ages. We don't know for certain when this event will take place, but I believe this great disappearance will occur in time to deliver Jesus' followers from the Great Tribulation.

HOW CAN WE KNOW IF GOD WILL DELIVER US?
God is consistent; this is the way he has worked in the past. He has never pronounced judgment without providing a way of escape.   Second, the very nature of the Tribulation itself infers the absence of Jesus' followers. As mentioned in Chapter Two, another name for the Great Tribulation is "the time of Jacob's trouble." The events during those seven years, and particularly the last three and a half, focus primarily on the nation of Israel. Today there are followers of Messiah among all peoples of the world including the Jewish people. The New Testament portion of the Bible refers to this collective group of Jesus' followers as "the saints," or "the Church." The New Testament book of Revelation describes the events of the Tribulation in great detail. Whereas Revelation has much to say about the Church in the first three chapters, when it comes to the passages concerning the Great Tribulation, there is no mention of any "saints" being on the earth. The only picture we see of the "saints" during this time is in heaven (Revelation 7:9).

Third, Jesus warned his followers to watch and always be prepared for his coming deliverance because they could not know when it would be.

Therefore you also be ready, for the Son of Man is coming at an hour you do not expect (Luke 12:40).

As we saw in Chapter Two, the prophet Daniel gave a very specific account of the timing of the Great Tribulation. That account includes how King Messiah will come to rescue Israel at the conclusion of the Great Tribulation. (More to come about that.) It stands to reason that followers of the Messiah would know what to expect and when to expect it, once these tribulation events begin to unfold. Therefore, if "the saints" are to be taken by surprise, it makes sense that it would be prior to the Great Tribulation.

Finally, God has specifically promised to deliver all those who walk with him today just as he delivered Noah and Lot. The Bible guarantees and promises those who trust in Messiah that they will be saved from wrath. And wrath is exactly what God will be pouring out upon the earth during the Great Tribulation. If you become a follower of Y'shua (Jesus), the Bible says you will not endure that wrath.

For God did not appoint us to suffer wrath but to receive salvation through our Lord Jesus Christ (1 Thessalonians 5:9).

Jesus the Messiah lived a perfect life and died as an offering for our sins. The plan God offers requires us to trust Jesus as our way of escape from judgment and follow him. When we do, we have a place with him in eternity, regardless of what may come.

There is a future hope. We can make a course alteration and avoid those dark clouds that loom ahead. Perhaps the idea of a Rapture sounds strange and unbelievable to you. Perhaps it seems more like a plot from a science fiction film or a comic book. It might even seem just plain "over the top." No doubt the ark that Noah was building looked quite odd to those who saw it sitting there on dry ground. But when those rains came pouring down and the flood waters started rising, that ark made a world of sense.

Noah had faith to believe and obey God. We need that same kind of faith. Y'shua the Messiah is God's ark to deliver us from the coming flood of God's judgment. He invites you to come to him and escape the destruction that lies ahead. Don't wait until it is too late. Put your trust in him today. The prayer on page 129 can help you to do just that.

CHAPTER FOUR

THE CENTER OF THE UNIVERSE

What is the role of Israel in the end times?

"And it shall happen in that day that I will make Jerusalem a very heavy stone for all peoples; all who would heave it away will surely be cut in pieces, though all nations of the earth are gathered against it" (Zechariah 12:3).

When people hear the name Israel, most think of a place. But there is more to Israel than a location; Israel is also a people, the Jewish people. The Bible talks about Israel as both a chosen people and a chosen place. This begs the question, "Chosen for what?" Many Jews facing persecution and suffering have echoed the sentiment of Tevye, the beloved milkman from *Fiddler on the Roof:* "Lord, maybe you could just choose someone else for a change?" The history of persecution—most notably the devastating tragedy of the Holocaust—makes it difficult to see how being "the chosen people" has benefited our people at all.

Likewise, it is difficult to imagine Jerusalem as the center of the universe. From a modern perspective, many cities seem

more likely choices: New York or London, Washington, D.C. or
Beijing, Moscow or Paris. But Jerusalem? Yet, clearly this little
patch of land remains the center of more attention and
controversy than any other place on the planet. The Bible
indicates that this will be so until the very end of the world.
God funneled his plan and purpose for this planet into one tiny
nation and then expanded it for all to see—in the place and the
people of Israel. When he brings that great plan to fruition, the
Land and people of Israel will be even more central in world
events than they are now!

GOD'S PROMISES TO ISRAEL

God's dealings with Israel have always been based on a
covenant. A covenant is a treaty, a binding and permanent
agreement. Israel's "chosenness" is based on just such a
covenant: the Abrahamic Covenant, so named because God
made this treaty with Abraham.

> The LORD had said to Abram, "Get out of your country,
> from your family and from your father's house, to a land
> that I will show you. I will make you a great nation; I will
> bless you and make your name great; and you shall be a
> blessing. I will bless those who bless you, and I will curse
> him who curses you; and in you all the families of the
> earth shall be blessed" (Genesis 12:1-3).

Gazing across the span of human history, it is plain to see
that God has kept his end of the bargain, which entailed a
threefold promise. The three aspects of that promise were
personal, national and universal.

First, God promised something personal to Abraham—to
make his name great—and so it is to this day. Three major
religions of this world—Judaism, Christianity and Islam—all
honor and revere the name of Abraham.

Second, God promised to make a great nation from
Abraham, and so he did. Despite the plots of Haman, Herod,

Hitler and Hussein throughout history, the Jewish nation survives and thrives.

Finally, God promised that all peoples of the earth would be blessed by Abraham. This too, has certainly been the case. The Jewish people have been the ones to transmit a knowledge of the one true God (monotheism) to rest of the world. The Scriptures, both Old and New Testament portions, serve as the foundation for the ethics and jurisprudence of Western civilization. All the writers of these books (with the possible exception of one New Testament writer) were Jewish. Many, many people in the world would attest that their Savior, the Messiah Jesus, also came through the Jewish people. Much more can be and has been said of the blessing of Abraham's offspring to the world.

The same God who made and kept that threefold promise also gave to Abraham and his Jewish descendants the Land we now call Israel (see Genesis 13:14-17).

God staked his own reputation on the survival and security of the Jewish people in the Land. That promise however did not insulate the people of Israel from their own failures. In fact, God also promised that if they failed to obey him and follow his commandments they would be exiled from the Land for many years. He warned that only a few would survive among the nations to which they would be driven (see Deuteronomy 4:25-27).

Diaspora: the exile of the Jewish people from the Land. The word sounds so removed, so clinical. But it was up close and personal for the Jewish people. First the Assyrians, then the Babylonians, and finally the Romans became instruments of the judgment God had promised the Jewish people. As the prophets foretold, the Jewish people were driven out of the Land and dispersed among the nations of the world. God is true to his word; he holds back neither the blessings nor the judgments he promises. Nevertheless, the positive aspects of God's promise concerning the Land and the people of Israel stand as an unconditional covenant for all time. And his

promise to bring his people back to the Land of Israel remained
a bright hope during even the darkest days of the Diaspora.

"Therefore behold, the days are coming," says the LORD,
"that it shall no more be said, 'The LORD lives who brought
up the children of Israel from the land of Egypt,' but, 'The
Lord lives who brought up the children of Israel from the
land of the north and from all the lands where He had
driven them.' For I will bring them back into their land
which I gave to their fathers" (Jeremiah 16:14,15).

This prophecy is being fulfilled today! Jewish people
continue to stream back to the Land of Israel, from the lands of
the north, from Russia and Ukraine. They are returning from
Ethiopia and South Africa, the United States and Canada, from
all the countries of the world where they have been
scattered. Never before has such a thing happened in the
history of the world. What other nation, after being defeated
and scattered throughout the world, has reconstituted itself and
regained self-determination in the land from which they were
scattered? This has happened with the Jewish people only
because God made a treaty with Abraham and vowed to keep
his promises for all time.

All of the events concerning Israel and the Jewish people
seem to be setting the stage for what the Bible describes as the
"end times." Everything God promised to Abraham has come to
pass. Therefore, we can be certain that what he says about the
future hope of Abraham's descendants will take place as well.

PROMISED PROBLEMS
Sadly, the Bible does not predict an easy future for Israel.
Most who have returned to the Land in our generation, did not
do so as faith-filled descendants of Abraham, but in unbelief.
God is regathering his chosen people not for glory, but for
judgment. Yes, the Bible predicts a bright hope for Israel in the
final analysis, but first comes the time of judgment described in

Chapter Two as the Great Tribulation.

That tribulation, as devastating as it will be, does not spell the destruction of the Jewish people: "Alas! For that day is great, so that none is like it; and it is the time of Jacob's trouble, *but he shall be saved out of it*" (Jeremiah 30:7, emphasis supplied). The good news is, as the prophet said, that Israel will be delivered in the end. The bad news is, that deliverance comes at enormous cost and through great conflict. The Land and the people of Israel will be ground zero, center stage of world attention, and that is precisely where God's final interventions in world history will occur. The people of Israel will be key players in this end-of-the-world scenario. They will be subjected to invading armies under the command of their sworn enemy, known as the Antichrist (more about him in the next chapter). The battles that will rage in the Land will be fierce and deadly as all the nations of the world will come against Jerusalem. Though the nations will eventually lose the war, the casualties of the battles will be even more devasting than those of the Holocaust:

> "And it shall happen in that day that I will make Jerusalem a very heavy stone for all peoples; all who would heave it away will surely be cut in pieces, though all nations of the earth are gathered against it. And it shall come to pass in all the land," says the LORD, "that two-thirds in it shall be cut off and die, but one-third shall be left in it: I will bring the one-third through the fire, will refine them as silver is refined, and test them as gold is tested. They will call on My name, and I will answer them. I will say, 'This is My people'; and each one will say, 'The LORD is my God'" (Zechariah 12:3; 13:8,9).

Zechariah predicts a staggering level of fatalities in this final conflict. But in the end, those who survive will return to God. When that happens, there will be a spiritual renewal of the people of Israel, the likes of which the world has never seen.

The Jewish people will become God's great emissaries in proclaiming to all the world the message of hope and faith in the coming Messiah.

As was pointed out in Chapter One, even though many thousands of Jewish people embraced Jesus in the first century, theirs was the minority opinion within Israel. And so it has remained to this day. However, all that is about to change.

JEWISH PREACHERS

God's covenant with Abraham promised ultimate blessing to all the world through Abraham's descendants. How ironic that the majority of Jewish people have not themselves received the greatest blessing that they brought to others: the Messiah Jesus. But the time is coming when Israel will not only embrace Y'shua, they will become the greatest evangelists for their Messiah the world has ever seen. Think about it. God used a minority of Jews who believed in Jesus to turn the first-century world upside down with an amazing message of hope and life. Is it possible that in the last days, God will again empower Jewish people with that message of hope and life in Jesus? I believe so.

The Bible tells of two amazing groups of Jewish people who will carry this message of judgment and salvation in Y'shua. The first group is a duo; a pair of individuals known as "the two witnesses." (You can read about them in Chapter Five.)

The second group of Jewish people is the key to worldwide end time spiritual revival. This group is known as "the 144,000."

The Bible tells us that at the beginning of the seven-year tribulation period the majority of the Jewish people will be deceived by the Antichrist, a charismatic leader who inspires trust and devotion from all quarters of the world. He will make a treaty with Israel, a treaty that he intends to break. But there is a significant minority of Jewish people who will not be deceived by the Antichrist. That group is the 144,000. There is a great deal of symbolism in the apocalyptic passages that describe them, but we do know concretely that these are Jewish people who believe in and follow Jesus, the Lamb of God:

> Then I heard the number of those who were sealed. One
> hundred and forty-four thousand from the tribes of Israel. . . .
> Then I looked, and behold, a Lamb standing on Mount
> Zion, and with Him one hundred and forty-four
> thousand, having His Father's name written on their
> foreheads. . . . These are the ones who follow the Lamb
> wherever He goes. These were redeemed from among
> men, being firstfruits to God and to the Lamb
> (Revelation 7:4; 14:1,4*b*).

The Jewish people in this passage represent all the tribes of
Israel. The portrayal of them having the name of the father and
of "the Lamb" on their foreheads refers to the fact that they
are sealed, that is, set apart by God during the tribulation
period as "first fruits." The term, "first fruits" is used
throughout the Bible to refer to the beginning of the harvest,
which is specially dedicated to God. In other words, the
144,000 represent the very beginning of God's work of
spiritual "harvest" among the whole nation of Israel, a harvest
whereby God will gather in the hearts of his people.

While the majority of the world will be deceived by the
Antichrist, this select group of Jewish people will stand against
him. They will boldly proclaim the message of the Lamb, Jesus
the Messiah. When the time comes for the Antichrist to betray
Israel, the nations of the world will gather to attack her. Then
the situation will be revealed for what it is. The 144,000 and
their message of hope will prove true in the sight of all of Israel
and the world. Jews and Gentiles alike will be able to respond
to God's message of hope during this dark time, but it will be
especially significant for the nation of Israel.

Up until this time, Israel experiences what Paul called, "a
partial blindness" in his address to the Gentile Christians in
Romans 11:25:

> For I do not desire, brethren, that you should be ignorant of
> this mystery, lest you should be wise in your own opinion,

that blindness in part has happened to Israel until the fullness of the Gentiles has come in.

In other words, a minority of Jewish people have been responding to the good news of Messiah as individuals, but from a national perspective Israel has not been able to see Jesus for who he is. Those of us who are Jewish believers in Jesus expect to be in the minority. That will begin to change with the coming of the two witnesses, and even more with the 144,000. The treachery and betrayal of the Antichrist and the swarming armies of the nations coming against her, will prepare Israel to respond, as a nation, to the message of hope in Y'shua.

And that is when all of the idolatry, all of the unbelief, all the blindness and hardness of heart will come to an end. Real salvation, physical and spiritual, will come to all of Israel. The clouds will roll back like a scroll and the Messiah himself will descend from Heaven to Jerusalem. And this time, *kol Israel,* all the people of Israel will recognize him, even as the prophet Zechariah predicted in the Hebrew Scriptures:

> "And I will pour on the house of David and on the inhabitants of Jerusalem the Spirit of grace and supplication; then they will look on Me whom they pierced. Yes, they will mourn for Him as one mourns for his only son, and grieve for Him as one grieves for a firstborn. . . . In that day a fountain shall be opened for the house of David and for the inhabitants of Jerusalem, for sin and for uncleanness" (Zechariah 12:10; 13:1).

In that greatest of all end times moments, God will rescue the Jewish people from her enemies and bring everlasting peace and justice on the earth.

In a sense, it will be a brand new beginning for Israel and the world. The people and the place of Israel will still have a central role to play (see Chapter Ten). But the center of the universe will not be the people or the place of Israel. The center of the universe will be the Messiah of Israel who comes to live and reign upon the earth.

The last public words that Jesus the Messiah said to the Jewish nation in Jerusalem before his death were, "You'll not see me again until you say 'Baruch haba bashem adonai'" (Blessed is he who comes in the name of the Lord). In the end, that is exactly what the nation of Israel will say to welcome back the King Messiah. But the Bible predicts there will be much suffering and death before that happens. There is no need to wait until then to welcome the Messiah Jesus. He is ready to reign in your life today.

Jews and Gentiles who believe Jesus' claims and welcome him as the blessed one who comes in the name of the Lord are now experiencing the joy, peace and forgiveness he will one day bring on a worldwide scale. If you are ready to believe and receive that joy and peace and forgiveness, you can do so by welcoming Jesus to be your Messiah and Lord right now. The prayer found on page 129 will help you to do just that.

CHAPTER FIVE

OUR MORTAL ENEMY

Who is the Antichrist?

*"He will become very strong, but not by his own power. He
will cause astounding devastation and will succeed in
whatever he does. He will destroy the mighty men and the
holy people" (Daniel 8:24).*

Of all Daniel's predictions, perhaps this one has inspired the
most speculation. A world leader is going to burst upon
the scene with great power and authority. He will be
immensely popular and win wide acclaim and admiration as a
wise man, a man of peace. He will use his popularity to deceive
many people and by the time they realize his treachery, it will
be too late. He will wreak havoc on the world. Enter the
Antichrist.

Many people spend a good deal of their time trying to figure
out who this Antichrist will be, or trying to persuade others of
what they think they've discovered about the Antichrist! I
doubt if Rev. Jerry Falwell is one of those people, and he
probably did not intend to create a major incident when he
casually mentioned, "... and of course he [the Antichrist] will be
Jewish ..." Well, the Associated Press picked up that quote and
charges of anti-Semitism began flying fast and furious. Most

Jewish leaders had little idea of who or what the Antichrist is, but this much they knew: It can't be any good to have people think that he's Jewish! I happen to disagree with Rev. Falwell's opinion about the origins of the Antichrist. The Bible is not clear who the Antichrist's people are, but we Jews have seen his type before and it seems highly unlikely that this destroyer of Jews would himself be a Jew (see Appendix 4).

ANTICHRIST AND HANUKKAH

To understand this treacherous character and what he stands for, we need to reflect on the story of Hanukkah.

It was approximately 165 B.C., and the Jewish people had been enjoying relative peace and tranquility in the Land of Israel, which had been divided between two of Alexander the Great's generals, Ptolemy and Seleucus. The story opens with the Seleucid ruler of Syria named Antiochus. Much of this history is recorded in the apocryphal book of Maccabees.

Soon it became apparent that Antiochus was intent on forced hellenization (imposing Greek culture and religion) and that meant eradicating belief in and worship of the God of Israel. Antiochus therefore forbade worship on the Sabbath, the rite of circumcision and the offering of Temple sacrifices. Further, he ordered the destruction of the Hebrew Scriptures. He commanded the Jews to eat forbidden (unclean) food and he erected numerous altars at which the Jews, under pain of death, were to offer unkosher sacrifices.

As if all this weren't enough, Antiochus dedicated an altar to Zeus in the Temple, and desecrated the holy altar by sacrificing a swine upon it. Finally, as he stood in the Temple, he declared himself to be "Epiphanes," or God manifested. He considered himself to be the incarnation of Zeus on earth and actually demanded that people worship him in place of the Almighty God. The festival of Hanukkah commemorates how the Jewish people rejected Antiochus and his false claims, and, with the help of God, defeated his armies and recaptured Jerusalem and the Temple.

The Hanukkah story serves as a precursor, or to use a

theological term, a "type" of the end times ruler known as the Antichrist. The term Antichrist is used sparingly in the Bible and does not always refer to this one specific end times figure. The term Antichrist points to one who opposes the Christ or Messiah. But in other places he is referred to as "the prince," "a king," "the man of lawlessness" or "the Beast."

The prophet Daniel peered into the future and saw Antiochus on the horizon of Israel's future. God revealed a glimpse of that evil king as a thunderstorm, a mere squall in comparison to the coming hurricane of the Beast. Listen to how he describes this most sinister of all banes:

He shall speak pompous words against the Most High, shall persecute the saints of the Most High, and shall intend to change times and law. Then the saints shall be given into his hand for a time and times and half a time.... A king shall arise, having fierce features, who understands sinister schemes. His power shall be mighty, but not by his own power; he shall destroy fearfully, and shall prosper and thrive; he shall destroy the mighty, and also the holy people. Through his cunning he shall cause deceit to prosper under his rule; and he shall exalt himself in his heart. He shall destroy many in their prosperity. He shall even rise against the Prince of princes; But he shall be broken without human means.... Then the king shall do according to his own will: he shall exalt and magnify himself above every god, shall speak blasphemies against the God of gods, and shall prosper till the wrath has been accomplished; for what has been determined shall be done. He shall regard neither the God of his fathers nor the desire of women, nor regard any god; for he shall exalt himself above them all (Daniel 7:25; 8:23-25; 11:36,37).

This vision of the Jewish prophet Daniel is quite frightening, the incarnation of evil on earth. If you believe the notion of a world leader like the Antichrist is too far-fetched to become a reality in our day please take a moment to consider: we have already seen eminently powerful and wicked rulers rise and wreak great havoc on the world. Adolph Hitler, Joseph Stalin and Pol Pot—these are some of the worst murderers and destroyers of all time. And they all lived in the same generation! Each was at one time admired, even adored by his nation. Each projected a magnetism that mesmerized people, articulated an ideology that mobilized people and created a machinery that manipulated an entire civilization.

THE EVIL FRONT MAN

How is it possible for such evil, such utter depravity to gain a foothold in the world? The Bible offers a simple explanation. This world is the scene of a vast unfolding cosmic battle between light and dark, between the forces of good and evil, between God and his adversary, also called Satan. This adversary, this Satan, is not a fictitious character like a Darth Vader from *Star Wars*. He is real and he is our mortal enemy. He is not an impish creature with pointy ears and a pitchfork. He is a powerful spiritual being, created as a beautiful angel. His rebellion against God before the creation of humankind has continued throughout our history. Satan's anger toward God is unleashed upon anything and everyone that God loves: people in general, and God's people in particular.

Satan's efforts to wreak havoc on the earth can be seen throughout history, and sadly, he has had many successes. His successes are not merely a matter of history, but a very real part of the future as well. World events are moving toward Satan's ultimate challenge. The Antichrist will be Satan's main instrument, his front man in the final climax of satanic rebellion against God. He won't be called the Antichrist. He will have a politically correct title. He will be known as a man of peace, a military genius, a philosopher. He will be clever, persistent, a great orator, highly intelligent, head and shoulders above the average person. This will be the man of the hour. And he will deceive people, turning them away from God, to godlessness. He's Satan's guy.

WHAT WILL HE DO?

What else do we know about him? How will we be able to recognize him? The prophet Daniel gives us the most important clues.

"He will confirm a covenant with many for one seven. In the middle of the seven, he will put an end to sacrifice and offering and on a wing of the temple he will set up an abomination that causes desolation until the end that is decreed is poured out on him" (Daniel 9:27).

His activities begin when he confirms a covenant or treaty with Israel. This event marks the beginning of the Tribulation, that seven-year period also known as the time of Jacob's trouble. That trouble is not immediately apparent. Undoubtedly this treaty is met with all the hope and fanfare accorded to a historic peace treaty. By implication, this Antichrist is a world ruler, perhaps even representing a coalition of world powers. Whatever his power base may be, he is in a position to negotiate a peace treaty with Israel.

Over the years many world leaders have made genuine efforts to establish peace in the Middle East. This world leader will appear to succeed where others have failed. However the appearance will be deceiving. His efforts will not be genuine. After three and one half years he will break the treaty and reveal his contempt for the nation of Israel. Just as his precursor Antiochus denigrated and defiled the Temple, the Antichrist will do the same (more about that in the next chapter).

As with Hitler, the destruction of the Jewish people is only part of the Antichrist's plan; his ultimate goal is world domination. The book of Revelation adds important details to the portrait given us by Daniel:

And I saw a beast rising up out of the sea ... The dragon
gave him his power, his throne, and great authority. And I
saw one of the heads as if it had been mortally wounded,
and his deadly wound was healed. And all the world
marveled and followed the beast. So they worshiped the
dragon who gave authority to the beast; and they
worshiped the beast, saying, "Who is like the beast? Who
is able to make war with him?" (Revelation 13:1-4).

If Daniel leaves us in any doubt that this world ruler is the front
man for Satan, that doubt is laid to rest by this passage in
Revelation. The dragon is a metaphor for Satan, and it is he who
empowers the Beast. An extraordinary occurrence enables the
Antichrist to gain power and a worldwide following. First, he
receives a fatal wound, perhaps during an attempted assassination.
By all accounts, the Beast should be dead, but instead, the wound
is miraculously healed. And it seems this amazing event takes place
in view of the entire world, perhaps even on satellite television. In
any case, this supernatural event solidifies his worldwide power
base. "And all the world marveled and followed the Beast."

This miraculous power that brings the Beast back from the
dead zooms in on the spiritual nature of this cosmic conflict.
People begin to worship the Beast and the dragon who is the
source of his power. Now it is evident why the Beast is called
Antichrist. His supposed "resurrection" is the adversary's trump
card, a demonstration of tremendous power intended to steal
people's hearts and their worship of the one true God and his
resurrected Messiah. The gloves are off.

Perhaps the whole idea of resurrection seems foreign to you,
a Christian belief that has nothing to do with Jewish ideas about
God or the Messiah. However that is not the case. As recently
as 1994, with the death the Lubavitch rebbe, Menachem
Schneerson (hailed by many of his followers as the Messiah),
there was a flurry of anticipation and controversy over whether
or not he would be resurrected. Nor is the Lubavitch belief in
a possible resurrection of the Messiah an aberration from

traditional Judaism. Jewish religious scholars such as Israeli author and lecturer Pinchas Lapide, have maintained that resurrection is very much a Jewish concept. Rabbi Neil Gillman (who is not a believer in Jesus), is another example. He provided biblical and rabbinical background to show that resurrection is a viable concept in Judaism in his 1997 book, *The Death of Death: Resurrection and Immortality in Jewish Thought.*

So the seeming resurrection of the Antichrist gives him tremendous credibility, perhaps even among the people of Israel. After all, many first-century Jewish people who saw Jesus alive after his crucifixion believed his messianic claims. It is worth noting the parallel here, and also the divergence between the two resurrections. Both Jesus and the Antichrist demonstrate that death cannot hold them. In the case of Jesus, the New Testament says that he laid down his life willingly as an atonement for sin. The understanding is that God brought him back from the dead as a confirmation that he had lived a sinless life, and his sacrifice on behalf of humankind was acceptable. (More about the biblical significance of sacrifices in Chapter Six.)   Death could not hold Y'shua, and his resurrection signaled that all those who trust in his atoning sacrifice are free from the penalty of death as well. The result of Y'shua's death and resurrection is reconciliation with God.

The Antichrist, on the other hand, will have shown his contempt for God and his people by the time he is mortally wounded. He is not God's chosen, but Satan's chosen. And while Satan, as a powerful spiritual being, is able to work a miraculous healing to bring his front man back from the dead, he is not able, nor does he desire, to reconcile people with God. In fact, the resurrection of the Antichrist will have precisely the opposite purpose and effect.

THE ANTICHRIST AND HIS CO-CONSPIRATOR

Revelation describes the Antichrist as the Beast, but goes on to tell about another beast. He is the final member of what now appears to be an "unholy trinity":

Then I saw another beast, coming up out of the earth, . . .
He performs great signs, so that he even makes fire
come down from heaven on the earth in the sight of
men. . . . He causes all, both small and great, rich and
poor, free and slave, to receive the mark on their right
hand or on their foreheads, and that no one may buy or
sell except one who has the mark or the name of the
beast, for it is the number of a man: His number is 666
(Revelation 13:11–18).

This beast, also called "the false prophet," acts as an aide and
support for the Antichrist. He demonstrates supernatural
powers as well. But his main purpose seems to be the increase
of the Antichrist's worldwide domination, through economic
manipulation. He does this through a worldwide registry; all
people are required to have a mark imprinted on their right
hand and forehead in order to do business anywhere in the
world. This mark becomes the means of control over all the
nations of the world; the Bible indicates that it will be
impossible to carry on normal commerce without it.

What exactly is this mark? There's been plenty of
speculation. It may be some kind of scannable infrared mark
rather than a visible sign. Some people have wondered if it has
something to do with credit cards or some kind of digital
identification. But the Bible seems to indicate that it is more
like a passport than a credit card. Credit cards give each person
a different number, according to his or her identity. The mark
of the Beast imposes the same number, his number, on
everyone. So what is the number? It is the number of the
Beast's name, 666.

Once again, many have speculated about the number as well,
but it is fairly straightforward. The Beast has a name and that
name has a certain number attributed to it. In Jewish tradition
there is a practice known as gematria whereby each Hebrew
letter has a particular number assigned to it. Words and names
can be represented by certain numbers based on the

corresponding numbers of the Hebrew letters used to spell them. For example, Jesus is the anglicized pronunciation of Y'shua. The number corresponding to the Hebrew letters for Y'shua would be 749. If one desired to attach symbolism to this, seven is the perfect number, the number of completion. Forty-nine is seven sevens, or perfection times perfection. The Antichrist's name is going to equal 666, which, if one wanted to attach symbolism to it, falls short of perfection on three counts. Having said all of that, we have no idea what the name of the Beast might be.

The Midrash, Jewish commentary from the Middle Ages, calls the Beast "Armillus." In fact, there are somewhere between ten and fifteen separate passages in post-biblical Jewish literature that speculate on this beast described in Daniel. He is portrayed as having one small eye and one large eye. He is said to be deaf in one ear, with arms drooping down below his knees. None of it sounds too appealing, but this beast is no laughing matter, especially for those who refuse to receive his mark. Many who choose to oppose him in this way will be murdered.

THE LOYAL OPPOSITION

Two of the most prominent martyrs will be the two witnesses mentioned in Chapter Four. An account of their deaths is given in the book of Revelation as well:

And I will give power to my two witnesses, and they will prophesy one thousand two hundred and sixty days, clothed in sackcloth. These have power to shut heaven, so that no rain falls in the days of their prophecy. . . . Now when they finish their testimony, the beast that ascends out of the bottomless pit will make war against them, overcome them, and kill them. . . . Then those from the peoples, tribes, tongues, and nations will see their dead bodies three and a half days, and not allow their dead bodies to be put into graves. And those who dwell on the earth will rejoice over them, make merry, and send gifts to one another, because these two prophets tormented those who dwell on the earth. Now after the three and a half days the breath of life from God entered them, and they stood on their feet, and great fear fell on those who saw them. And they heard a loud voice from heaven saying to them, "Come up here." And they ascended to heaven in a cloud, and their enemies saw them (Revelation 11:3,6*a*,7,9-12).

These are powerful witnesses who challenge the person and the message of the Antichrist. The passage does not clearly state that they are Jews but it seems likely that they are. They appear as Old Testament prophets in sackcloth, prophesying in Jerusalem. The miraculous powers they exercise hearken back to the great Jewish prophets of old, like Moses and Elijah. Some of the language may be figurative to emphasize the power that these witnesses have, but it would seem that they appear during the first part of the Tribulation, the first three and a half years. (Notice the mention of 1,260 days.) The judgment that comes upon the earth in the last three and a half years of tribulation will be more severe. The judgment God will pour out then will take into account the opportunity the world has to respond to the powerful ministry of these witnesses, and the fact that their response is to reject them.

Many people speculate about the identity of these two witnesses. Malachi 4:5 speaks about Elijah who will come before the "great and terrible day of the Lord." Some believe this verse indicates that one of these men will be Elijah. The Bible doesn't tell us who the witnesses are, except that they are specially anointed by God for specific and powerful service to him. Because they resist the Antichrist, and apparently speak against him in their prophecies, the Beast kills them and leaves their corpses to serve as an example to anyone who would challenge his authority. Those who follow the Beast and whose hearts are turned away from God are glad to have an end to their prophesying. But these witnesses have the last word, so to speak, because God brings them back to life, much to the fear and dismay of those who look on.

The murder of the two witnesses is representative of how the Antichrist persecutes Israel and all those who refuse his authority, with a ferocity unparalleled in world history. But in the end, there is a payback for the Antichrist and the false prophet:

> And then the lawless one will be revealed, whom the Lord will consume with the breath of His mouth and destroy with the brightness of His coming....Then the beast was captured, and with him the false prophet....These two were cast alive into the lake of fire burning with brimstone (2 Thessalonians 2:8; Revelation 19:20).

Regardless of all the terrifying havoc this conflict of all the ages will wreak on humanity, we can know today who wins in the end. I don't envy anyone who will have to endure those seven horrible years, but I can guarantee that God is in control and anyone who trusts him will ultimately prevail. He will crush the dragon and his front men. The anti-Messiah will lose out to the real Messiah, and the world will be finally liberated. If you happen to be around and witness the signing of a peace treaty with Israel, and some rather strange goings-on, you will know to begin counting time! Hopefully you will also choose to be on the winning side. You don't have to wait until the Antichrist shows up to do that. If you want the reconciliation and forgiveness the real Christ, Y'shua, came to give, you can have it today. The prayer on page 129 can help you as you make your decision.

CHAPTER SIX

THE ABOMINATION OF DESOLATION

What happens in the Temple?

"So when you see standing in the holy place 'the abomination that causes desolation,' then let those who are in Judea flee to the mountains" (Matthew 24:15,16).

The request reads: "Children wanted for future Temple service. Ultra-orthodox Jewish sect is searching for parents willing to hand over newborn sons to be raised in isolation and purity in preparation for the rebuilding of the biblical temple in Jerusalem. Only members of the Jewish priestly caste, the Kohanim need apply."

Words from an ancient scroll discovered in a recent archeological dig? Or perhaps an excerpt from a Hollywood screenplay for some biblical epic? Actually, those words are a simple advertisement from a March 1998 edition of the contemporary Israeli newspaper, *Haaretz*. What some westerners might consider ancient conflicts and antiquated concerns are, in fact, current events to many people in the

Middle East. And no subject is more controversial or fraught with more emotional TNT than rebuilding the Temple in Jerusalem.

If you or anyone you know has ever been to Israel you have probably seen the familiar view of Jerusalem from the eastern slope of the Mount of Olives. There, glistening in the sun, is the golden Dome of the Rock, and just to the south, the plainer looking El-Aksa Mosque. Both are recognized as holy sites for the religion of Islam, and they are built on top of the Temple Mount, Mount Moriah, which is the only truly holy site in all of Judaism. There, Solomon built the First Temple some 3000 years ago. There, Ezra rebuilt the Second Temple 2500 years ago. And there, thousands of religious Jews hope and pray and work for the rebuilding of what will be the Third Temple in Jerusalem (see appendix 5).

Why should the idea of rebuilding the Temple stir such passion and kindle such hopes and dreams? Why is this ancient edifice so important to our people today? The answer lies back in the earliest period of Jewish history, back in the days of Abraham and Isaac.

ABRAHAM, ISAAC AND THE TEMPLE MOUNT

Genesis 22 records what is known as "the Akedah," or the binding of Isaac: the event in which the Lord commanded Abraham to sacrifice his son Isaac on a mountain in the land of Moriah. Abraham journeyed up that mountain with Isaac in obedience to God's command. When Isaac noted that there was wood and fire, but no animal for the sacrifice, his father replied, "God will provide." Abraham then built an altar and bound his son with cords on that altar. We are told that he actually had his knife poised to slay his son when the Angel of the Lord stopped him. God showed him a ram caught in the thicket by its horns. Abraham joyfully sacrificed that ram in place of his son, and called the place, "Yaveh Yireh," the Lord will provide. He declared, "In the mountain of the Lord it shall be provided" (Genesis 22:14).

God blessed Abraham for the tremendous faith he showed

in being willing to sacrifice his son, the son of promise for whom Abraham and Sarah had waited so long. He responded to Abraham's faith by promising to make his descendants like the stars of the heavens. That event has been central to Jewish and Christian theology ever since. For many Jewish people, the main point is that God did not approve of or want human sacrifices such as the surrounding pagan nations performed.

Yet this passage does not seem to be about those pagan practices. Both Jews and Christians recognize the mountain on which the Akedah took place as the mountain of God, the place where it was said, "the Lord will provide."

GOD'S PROMISE CONCERNING THE TEMPLE

Centuries later, as the Jewish nation wandered in the wilderness, Moses envisioned a sanctuary where God's presence would one day dwell. At that time, Israel had the Tabernacle, a portable place of worship for a wandering people. It showed God's commitment to be with his people while they were yet homeless. But just as God had promised the people of Israel a home, so there would be a permanent place for him to dwell in their midst. Moses himself prayed for such a place:

> You will bring them in and plant them in the mountain of Your inheritance, in the place, O Lord, which You have made for Your own dwelling, the sanctuary, O Lord, which Your hands have established (Exodus 15:17).

Moses envisioned the mountain of inheritance—the place where Abraham's faith in God's provision was tested and blessed—as the ideal place for the sanctuary of God.

The great significance of the Tabernacle and eventually the Temple was God's promise to Israel concerning these places:

> "And there I will meet with you, and I will speak with you from above the mercy seat, from between the two cherubim which are on the ark of the Testimony, about

everything which I will give you in commandment to the children of Israel. . . . This shall be a continual burnt offering throughout your generations at the door of the tabernacle of meeting before the Lord, where I will meet you to speak with you. And there I will meet with the children of Israel, and the tabernacle shall be sanctified by My glory" (Exodus 25:22; 29:42,43).

These promises were the pillars of what would be accomplished in the Temple. First, God promised to be present. Second, God promised to provide.   God would dwell in the midst of his people and speak with them. He would provide atonement for their sins, forgive them and make them holy. That atonement was secured through the blood of the animal sacrifices offered on the altar.

THE SYMBOLISM OF THE SACRIFICES
Such sacrifices may strike modern minds as strange, even barbaric. But the system was rich in symbolism and significance for Israel because of God's command: "For the life of the flesh is in the blood, and I have given it to you upon the altar to make atonement for your souls; for it is the blood that makes atonement for the soul" (Leviticus 17:11).

These sacrifices were a way of acknowledging the consequence of disobeying God. That consequence was death. God has zero tolerance for sin. But God's righteousness and judgment are tempered by his other perfections, especially his mercy and grace. The sacrifices provided a way for him to extend that mercy and grace—by allowing a substitute. The animal died in place of the transgressor, and at no small cost to the one who offered the sacrifice, either.

In an agrarian economy, those animals were expensive and were not lightly given in sacrifice. The whole event was a drama of the highest order in Israel's religious life. The stage that God provided for this drama was the Tabernacle and later, the Temple. Only in these holy places would God allow this

most profound experience. The Tabernacle, and eventually the
Temple, was Israel's heartbeat, the center of her encounter with
God's presence and provision of atoning power.

GOD'S PRESENCE IN THE TEMPLE
It was hundreds of years before Moses' prayer for a sanctuary
was answered. King David had wanted to build the Temple on
that very place where Abraham offered up Isaac; he even
bought the property on Mt. Moriah in Jerusalem from a man
named Arunah. But God prevented him from building the
Temple. Instead he appointed Solomon, David's son, to build
the Temple on Mt. Moriah. When the time came to dedicate the
Temple, God fulfilled Moses' prophecy concerning this
sanctuary. God came to dwell there.

> And it came to pass, when the priests came out of the
> holy place that the cloud filled the house of the LORD so
> that the priests could not continue ministering because of
> the cloud; for the glory of the LORD filled the house of the
> LORD (1 Kings 8:10,11).

What a powerful moment in the religious life of the nation.
There could be no doubt that the Temple was now the center
of Israel's worship and the anchor of her religious sensibility.

THE TRAGEDY OF THE TEMPLE
That first Temple stood for nearly 400 years. But the problem
was, the Jewish people began to put their confidence in the
Temple itself rather than the One who dwelt in the Temple. It
was as though the people thought they had God's power
harnessed within the confines of the building—even though
they were no longer worshipping him but had turned to idols.
God warned that judgment was coming and in 586 B.C. that
judgment came in the form of the Babylonian conquerors. The
Temple of the LORD in all of its beauty was destroyed.
Words can't describe the agony of that experience in Israel's

history. In a sense, her "kishkes" were ripped out. Her awareness of calling and purpose was rooted in that Temple and in the knowledge that God was in her midst. With no Temple, there was no assurance of God's presence or his provision of forgiveness for the nation.

In 538 B.C., Zerubbabel and a host of Israelites returned from their captivity in Babylon to Jerusalem in accordance with the decree of King Cyrus of Persia. The prophet Ezra oversaw the building of the Second Temple, which was completed 23 years later. But the Second Temple hardly compared to the first. It was approximately the same size, but not nearly as ornate. What is more, there seems to have been no Ark of the Covenant in the Most Holy Place. There was only emptiness, with nothing covering the now famous foundation stone. And the very glory of God so evident in the First Temple seemed absent as well.

In fact, according to the Roman historian Tacitus, when the Roman general Pompeii visited Jerusalem, he marched right into the Temple and into the Most Holy Place. He came back out and declared to the Jews in astonishment, "It's empty. There's nothing there but darkness." And of course, he was right. Later (beginning in 19 B.C.), Herod attempted to restore the Temple to some of its former beauty. The work continued for some 82 years.

JESUS AND THE TEMPLE

Many of Jesus' activities and teachings took place in and around that Temple. Actually, he made some of his most controversial comments concerning it: "Jesus answered and said to them, 'Destroy this temple, and in three days I will raise it up.' Then the Jews said, 'It has taken forty-six years to build this temple, and will You raise it up in three days?' But He was speaking of the temple of His body" (John 2:19–21).

By identifying himself as the Temple, Jesus was claiming to fulfill the very purpose of that Temple. In one brief, yet profound, statement he claimed to represent the very presence of God once so evident in the Temple.

Jesus identified himself, not only with the Temple, but with the Temple sacrifice. What God did not require Abraham to do in sacrificing his son Isaac, God himself did in sending his son Jesus to die on a cross. An outlandish claim? It would have been had the second part of Jesus' prediction not come true. But he did rise from the dead after three days, as promised, proving that his sacrifice for sin was acceptable once and for all. Followers of Jesus believe that this was God's plan all along, and that the animal sacrifices pointed to a time when an innocent person, God's own son, would willingly take the punishment for the sins of the people: something that an animal could never do.

But Jesus also made an ominous prediction concerning that Second Temple which, if true, would authenticate what he had said all along about his own life and work.

> Then Jesus went out and departed from the temple, and His disciples came up to show Him the buildings of the temple. And Jesus said to them, "Do you not see all these things? Assuredly, I say to you, not one stone shall be left here upon another, that shall not be thrown down" (Matthew 24:1,2).

Jesus clearly predicted the destruction of the Second Temple. Titus and his Roman legions fulfilled that prediction as they marched into Jerusalem, destroyed the city and destroyed the Temple. This national tragedy for Israel pointed back to the claims of Jesus of Nazareth. Thousands of Jews had already placed their faith in Y'shua. At the destruction of that Second Temple in A.D. 70, thousands more did so as well. Yet most of my Jewish people did not. And so it remains to this day.

The Temple is hardly a daily concern to the majority of Jewish people today. On June 7, 1967, Israeli troops moved into the Old City and took control of the Temple Mount. That was a historic event of immense proportion. For the first time in some 2000 years, Jews were in a position to rebuild the

Temple. Nevertheless, about ten days later, Moshe Dayan took down the Israeli flag and returned the Temple Mount to Muslim control. Israel's secular military leaders had no commitment to rebuilding the Temple. To them it was a relic of the past. To them, the Temple Mount represented potential conflict with Islam, more of a political liability than anything else. Many Jews today feel quite differently about that "little" piece of real estate.

A FUTURE TEMPLE

The hope for the rebuilding of the Temple in Jerusalem has never been extinguished. The daily synagogue prayers have kept that hope alive. "Be pleased, Lord our God, with Thy people Israel and with their prayer. Restore the worship of Thy most holy sanctuary." This prayer, as articulated in the 18th benediction from the *Shmoneh Esre,* has been on the lips of Jewish people for 2000 years.

Will that prayer be answered? Is there a rebuilt Temple in Israel's future? The Bible clearly states that there will be a Temple in the end times. The Hebrew Scriptures and the New Testament both refer to that Temple, and to tragic events that will occur there in the last days. First the prophet Daniel, and then Jesus (referring to Daniel's prophecy) warned people about "the abomination that causes desolation standing in the holy place."

Up until recently, it seemed patently absurd that there could ever be a Third Temple in which this prophecy could be fulfilled. Now, however, despite the fact that two Muslim mosques sit upon the Temple Mount, there are Jewish groups concerned with training priests for the day that the Temple is restored. *Aterah Kohanim* is one such group. They have purchased many of the Arab homes in the Old City of Jerusalem, very near the Temple Mount. They have also set up *yeshivas* to educate and train Temple priests; two hundred men are in active training for the priesthood there now. Project Cornerstone is another group that raises funds to aid in training priests for the Temple.

Then there is the *Temple Mount Faithful,* a group that is ready to commence building at any moment. They've cut a massive piece of limestone, a 4.5-ton cornerstone to begin their work. Their first attempt to bring it up to the Temple Mount was in 1989. Each year during Sukkot, the Feast of Tabernacles, they enact the elaborate water-drawing ceremony at the pool of Siloam, and then attempt to set the cornerstone for the rebuilding of the Temple. Each year the Israeli government authorities prevent them. The site remains a holy place for Muslims and it is under Islamic control. Israeli government officials have little stomach for actions that might well lead to riots, or perhaps even World War III. However, there may be a solution for that barrier to rebuilding.

You see, recently some archaeologists have concluded that the actual location of the foundation stone upon which the ark once rested is north of the Dome of the Rock. If true, it is theoretically possible to rebuild the Temple without having to tear down the Muslim holy sites. Nevertheless, because of the proximity to the mosques, it remains a sensitive issue to say the least.

We can only speculate how the problems facing the rebuilding of the Temple will be resolved. In any case, the eagerness of religious Jews to see the Temple rebuilt—and the eagerness of many Christians, too, for that matter—does not take into account the fearsome events the Bible promises will occur surrounding this Temple.

BETRAYAL IN THE TEMPLE

Remember, the prophet Daniel tells us that the terrible time of tribulation begins with a peace treaty signed between Israel and the individual known as the Antichrist. Perhaps the treaty will actually clear the way for the rebuilding of the Temple. Anyone who could facilitate such a momentous accomplishment would be sure to win the respect and trust of many Israelis and religious Jews worldwide. Regardless of the nature of the treaty, whatever respect and trust it engendered will be betrayed within three and one half years. This betrayal will be manifested in such an insidious manner that Daniel could only describe it as the "abomination."

Imagine the joy of so many religious Jews when this Third Temple is built. Even among the secular Israelis of the day there will be a large measure of national pride in the elaborate structure built as a result of this peace treaty. Can you picture it? Money has poured in from all over the world to erect another wonder of the world. After over 2000 years, the Jewish priesthood is once again functioning in Jerusalem. Next scene: it all comes crashing down in a single act of horrific blasphemy. This man the Bible calls the Antichrist has become more than a formidable political ruler. He is receiving the adulation and worship of people around the world. He has come to expect it, demand it! He arrogantly enters the Temple his peace treaty helped make possible. "Worship me here," he demands. And he horrifies all of Israel with the Abomination of Desolation.

The utter desolation the Antichrist will cause will be unprecedented. We don't know the exact nature of the abomination, but it will make Antiochus (the precursor to the Antichrist), look like a friend of the Jews and it will be the beginning of a murderous rampage. The acts of Adolph Hitler and his SS troops will pale in comparison to the desolation caused by the Antichrist and his henchmen. A full two-thirds of the population of Israel will perish in the ensuing conflict, according to Zechariah 13:8. The hope of the Jewish people in seeing the glorious Temple rebuilt will, in fact, lead to their greatest calamity and suffering.

Those who understand this teaching of Scripture will temper their eagerness to see the Temple rebuilt with the realization that it will one day set the stage for Israel's darkest hour. But again, the saying holds true that it is darkest just before dawn. The Bible does prophesy the dramatic rescue of Israel by the one who declared, "Destroy this temple and in three days I will raise it up."

Y'shua, Jesus, will fulfill all the hope and promise that Israel could have and more. One day he will return to Jerusalem and put an end to the desolation caused by the Antichrist. In that day, all of Israel, and in fact, the whole world will realize their need for him. But he is always ready and waiting to bring God's presence and his provision of atonement to all who put their faith in him.

If you have experienced the desolation of knowing that life apart from God is devoid of any lasting meaning, and you want to be reconciled to him, he offers you that reconciliation today in the person of Y'shua, Jesus the Messiah. If you want to experience God's forgiveness, if you want to know his presence in your life, why not take the time now to invite Y'shua to be your Messiah and Savior from sin. If you need help to do that, turn to the prayer on page 129.

CHAPTER SEVEN

THE MOTHER OF ALL WARS

What is the Battle of Armageddon?

"And they gathered them together to the place called in Hebrew, Armageddon" (Revelation 16:16).

In an interview Malcolm Muggeridge had with Joseph Stalin's daughter, Svetlana, she described her last memory of her infamous father. The setting was his deathbed and she recalls how the last thing he did on this earth was raise himself up on that deathbed and with what strength he had remaining, shake his fist at the heavens. Then he lay down and died. Stalin, once a seminary student, had turned against religion with a hatred so deep that it fueled a brutal reign of terror in which he murdered 15 million of his countrymen. That hatred characterized him not only in life, but in death.

THE BEGINNING OF THE BATTLE

In order to understand the end times battle known as "Armageddon," we need to see it in context. This is not some isolated event in human history; it is really the culmination of a very old, long and drawn out battle.

The Psalmist wrote:

> Why do the nations rage, and the people plot a vain thing? The kings of the earth set themselves, and the rulers take counsel together, against the LORD and against His Anointed, saying, "Let us break their bonds in pieces and cast away their cords from us" (Psalm 2:1-3).

Stalin demonstrated what was in his heart with his dying breath. Tragically, that heart attitude can be found in everyone at one time or another: wholesale commitment to rebellion against our maker.

What provokes rebellion against God? Why do people work themselves into a frenzy trying to wrest control from an all-powerful God? The consequences of that rebellion are devastating; and will ultimately lead to the mother of all wars. In order to understand this, we need to go all the way back to *Gan Eden,* the garden of Eden, all the way back to the creation of the human race.

WHERE DID WE GO WRONG?

A rebellion of cosmic and tragic proportions occurred when the greatest of all the angelic beings, "Lucifer," the morning star, turned his back on his creator. Instead of accepting the honor of being the greatest and most powerful of God's servants, Lucifer chose to challenge the authority of the One who made him and all the worlds. He became *ha satan,* which is Hebrew for "the adversary." God cast this former angel of light down to the earth in judgment.

The Almighty could have easily destroyed his adversary. Satan had demonstrated all of the arrogance of a created being telling its creator, "I don't need you and you don't have the right to tell me what to do." God could have answered this challenge of sheer *chutzpah* by squashing Satan like a bug. But the Almighty had no need to prove his power; he was more interested in proving something else.

Satan had, by his actions, shouted to the universe that pride was acceptable and independence from God desirable. God decided to allow that pride, that independence, to run its course. Satan eventually would prove to himself, and to the world, that rebellion against God can only lead to meaninglessness, evil, pain and death. At the same time, God would enact his own plan which would dramatically demonstrate his love and grace. The King of the Universe would one day show the superiority of his ways very personally, humbling himself to a life of dependence and servanthood by becoming a man. And in becoming a man, he would redeem the human race.

Why would we need a redeemer? Simply because we allowed ourselves to be duped. Our first ancestors were seduced by Satan into believing that God did not really have their best interests at heart, and that rebelling against him was the only way to get what they really wanted and deserved. Things haven't changed much. The attitude of the human race ever since has been that really, we do not need God, that we can do just as well or better at deciding what is right, what is wrong and how we should live our lives. Even those who claim to believe and obey God say otherwise by their actions at various times in their lives. Since the tragic decision Adam and Eve made in the garden, no human being has ever managed to relate to God wisely and well on a consistent basis, living in complete trust and obedience throughout his or her whole life.

Ironically, because of our inflated pride in our own abilities and our lack of trust in God, we rip ourselves away from the one who knows and loves us the best. The whole fabric of our souls unravels. We may try to recut the cloth or reshape ourselves so we can somehow be satisfied without God, but it just doesn't work. When we human beings are out of sync with God, we quickly fall out of sync with one another, manipulating and trying to exert power over one another in the mistaken notion that we are or deserve to be in control of reality. When we make ourselves the highest authority, we demonstrate how

low we can sink. We become trapped by our own
shortcomings and unable to enjoy the relationship we were
meant to have with God and with the rest of creation. That is
the heart of our rebellion.

GOD'S RESPONSE TO REBELLION

We may not think we are rebelling against God; we may not
even believe God exists, but that too is rebellion, a decision not
to know what is readily available for us to know. God has
provided enough evidence for anyone who genuinely wants
the truth to know that he exists. And if God exists, then by
definition he knows far better than we do what is right and
how best we can have meaning and dignity and joy in our lives.
All two-year-old children will try to impose their desires and
expectations onto their parents. Caring fathers and mothers
don't allow their children to eat everything they want to put in
their little two-year-old mouths. They don't shrug and look the
other way when their little ones stumble toward the fireplace,
stretching their hands out gleefully to touch the pretty flames.

Some might find the comparison demeaning, and it's not to
say that God patronizes or treats us all like we are two-year-olds.
But even though God regards us as fully grown adults, consider
this: the gap between your understanding and a two-year-old's
understanding of his best interests is nothing compared to the
difference between God's understanding of your best interests
and your own understanding of the same. If you are a parent,
you are a "co-creator" of a human life. But God has created all
human life. He is the architect and builder of the universe. He
designed, mapped out and knows every single detail of how our
bodies, our intellects and our emotions work. He is father and
mother, the One without whom none of us would exist.

Some people don't know what it's like to have a parent who
understands how to love his or her children. Even the very best
parents make mistakes, and so the very worst can be pretty bad.
But God is the ideal parent. He knows how to be in a loving
relationship with us, how to care for, nurture and protect us, while

allowing us to stretch, to grow and to learn to be ourselves. He is more "for us" than any earthly parent could possibly be. We are at our best and most fulfilled when we are receptive to that relationship with him. Yet it is our nature to push God away, to assert our independence and insist that our rights outweigh God's. That is what is in our rebellious heart—pride and disobedience.

Part of God's whole plan is to show this rebellion for what it really is, to let people have their fill of sin and allow it to run its course. Eventually he will put an end to it. In the allegorical work, *The Great Divorce,* C. S. Lewis, says that Heaven is where the person who says, "God, your will be done" spends eternity. Hell is a place where God has finally said to an unrepentant rebel, "Fine—*your* will be done." Lewis portrays Hell as a place where the door is locked from the inside and where God has agreed to be locked out of people's lives—forever.

Ultimately, we end up choosing our own destinies. Most individuals end up choosing, however consciously or unconsciously, along with the nations the Psalmist wrote about, those who rage against the LORD and his anointed. Most do not realize that their choice has aligned them with the source of rage and rebellion, Satan. He must know who will win in the end, yet he is so filled with hate that he fights on so as to cause as much pain and destroy as many lives as possible, dragging as many people down with him as he can. As John Milton wrote in *Paradise Lost,* Satan's attitude seems to be, "It's better to rule in Hell than to serve in Heaven."

Eventually God must put his foot down (so to speak) and squash this age-old rebellion. The Bible says it will happen in the battle of Armageddon.

THE WAR TO END ALL WARS
Throughout Scripture, the end times, and particularly the battles, are described in what is known as apocalyptic language, prose which uses a great deal of symbolism. Animals are often used to represent people or nations, and especially those in leadership. Cosmic signs in the heavens are symbolic of

supernatural phenomena. The symbols can be taken literally in the sense that they point us to actual future events, but they are still symbols, and therefore not literal representations of those future events. Biblical phrases like, "the moon turning to blood," paint a picture of events and they point us to a deeper meaning, a theological meaning, if you will.

The perspective of the apocalypse appears pessimistic. Things are bad and they're going to get worse. But always, with this pessimistic attitude, there is a contrasting sense of future hope. There is a promise of salvation. The war is coming, the battle is going to be fierce and unavoidable, but there is a promise of deliverance in the midst of all the conflict. There is a transcendent reality, a promise, a certainty, that the Bible conveys. That reality, that promise is that God is in control. God will ensure that no matter how bad things get on earth, they will not get so bad that all hope is lost.

The final battle is actually a series of battles that begin during the seven-year Great Tribulation with what is known as the Battle of Gog and Magog.

> Now the word of the LORD came to me, saying, "Son of man, set your face against Gog . . . and prophesy against him, and say, 'Thus says the LORD GOD: "Behold, I am against you, O Gog, the prince of Rosh, Meshech, and Tubal" . . . After many days you will be visited. In the latter years you will come into the land of those brought back from the sword and gathered from many people on the mountains of Israel, which had long been desolate; they were brought out of the nations, and now all of them dwell safely. You will ascend, coming like a storm, covering the land like a cloud, you and all your troops and many peoples with you'" (Ezekiel 38:1,2,8,9).

Ezekiel paints a picture of a massive army descending upon the Land of Israel. The troops are led by Gog who is the leader of the land of Magog along with the other lands of Rosh,

Meshech and Tubal. Although these names are mentioned in Genesis 10 as sons of Japheth, we have a strong indication of which nations they represent today. Magog, Meshech and Tubal were tribes of the ancient world between the Black and Caspian Seas, which today is southern Russia. The tribes of Meshech and Tubal have given their names to cities of today, Moscow and Tobolsk. Rosh is believed by some to be where the name "Russia" came from.

When you consider that Moscow is almost a straight line due north from Jerusalem, it could very well be that a confederation of nations led by Russia are behind this first Tribulation battle. Ezekiel tells us that three other countries join with them: Persia, Ethiopia and Put. We know that Persia is Iran. The others appear to be African nations, perhaps including Libya. Together these nations attack the Land of Israel in the mountains of Israel. Their armies are placed from the northern end of the valley of Jezreel down into the areas of the south, Beer Sheva and the Negev. Jerusalem is in the middle of these mountains, and this is where the armies converge in a massive invasion.

The Bible says that these armies will cover the land just like a storm cloud. Ezekiel depicts Israel as a nation of unwalled cities, vulnerable to her enemies. Israel's defenses will be lowered because she believes she will be protected by the treaty she signed with the Antichrist three and one half years earlier. But Israel is betrayed. The attack comes and the nations of the world stand back and watch. They expect to see Israel destroyed, but they discover that there is a far greater power fighting for Israel than the sum total of all the nations. The LORD God himself.

"I will call for a sword against Gog throughout all My mountains," says the LORD GOD. "Every man's sword will be against his brother. And I will bring him to judgment with pestilence and bloodshed; I will rain down on him, on his troops, and on the many peoples who are with

him, flooding rain, great hailstones, fire, and brimstone"
(Ezekiel 38:21,22).

There is going to be mass confusion among Israel's enemies
as God's earth-shattering, miraculous intervention strikes.
These people are going to be utterly slaughtered. In fact,
Ezekiel tells us it will take Israel seven months to clean up after
the battle. Even so, the battle of Gog and Magog is only the
prelude to this final battle, often referred to as Armageddon. It
demonstrates to Israel her folly in having trusted in the peace
treaty or in power or leaders other than God. She discovers that
the only one worth putting trust in is the LORD.

The supernatural defeat of the armies of Gog and Magog
serve as the pretext for the Antichrist to invade the Land of
Israel. He has succeeded in his plan for world domination.
Thanks to the manipulation of his partner, the false prophet, he
has an economic stranglehold on the world. Between the signs
and wonders performed by the false prophet and the
miraculous healing of a mortal wound the Antichrist received
during an assassination attempt, all the peoples of the world are
actually worshiping the Antichrist as some kind of a guru-god.
All the peoples, that is, except for the Jewish people. His
blasphemy in the Temple has made our people see the light and
they have turned away from him. The Antichrist thought that
the federation of Gog and Magog would do in the Jewish
nation, but he was wrong. So his ultimate plan for annihilating
Jews now comes into play. Finally, we arrive at the main event.
The campaign of Armageddon.

Armageddon is a combination of two words: *Har* meaning
mountain and *Megiddo*, which is an actual hill overlooking the
valley of Jezreel. Megiddo was one of the fortified cities of King
Solomon. Today, you can visit the ancient ruins of the city and
look out over the Jezreel Valley. Israel has a key military base
right there and there is the constant buzz of military aircraft
taking off and landing in the midst of the lush surroundings of
fertile farmland.

The Jezreel Valley is a place of great historic significance. Deborah and Barak were victorious over the Canaanites there, Gideon defeated the Midianites there, King Saul was slain there, Jehu killed Ahaziah there and King Josiah was slain by the Egyptians there. Even Napoleon Bonaparte marched past Megiddo in his effort to win the Middle East. This military genius called it the most natural battleground on the whole earth. It should be no surprise that the plain of Armageddon is a gathering place for the armies of the Antichrist.

While people commonly refer to the *battle* of Armageddon, the appropriate word is "war" or "campaign." The details are described in several books of the Bible such as Joel, Zechariah and Matthew, but particularly in the book of Revelation.

There are three groups of participants in this battle. The first is the Antichrist and his armies. The armies of the Antichrist are said to represent all the nations of the world, except perhaps for "the kings of the east" who make up the second group. When the Bible speaks about kings of the east, it usually refers to the Persian and Arab kings east of the Jordan. Some have speculated that these armies are from the far east—Asia, perhaps China. Whatever the case, these kings of the East join in a confederacy with the Antichrist against the nation of Israel. They come across the Euphrates River, which has been dried up, perhaps by a dam, to engage his armies in battle. The third group consists of the Jewish people who are living in Israel, trying to protect their homeland against this massive invasion.

The gathering of the armies on the plain of Megiddo or Armageddon appears to be the first of several stages in this final campaign. Imagine what it will be like for Israel at this time: a massive army gathers in the very center of the country. Armies are approaching from the east to join with them. If ever there might be a sense of dread and doom, Israel is experiencing it at this point.

The second stage is sudden and unexpected: the destruction of Babylon in modern-day Iraq. Perhaps this happens as the armies of the east come across the Euphrates River. The Bible doesn't clearly spell out how this occurs, but the fact that it does happen enrages the Antichrist and leads to a direct attack on Jerusalem. This is the third stage in the campaign of Armageddon. The attack on Jerusalem is ferocious and the city is actually overcome by the invading armies.

> For I will gather all the nations to battle against Jerusalem; the city shall be taken, the houses rifled, and the women ravished. Half of the city shall go into captivity, but the remnant of the people shall not be cut off from the city" (Zechariah 14:2).

There is terrible bloodshed as Jerusalem suffers horrible defeat. The main battleground is in the valley of Jehoshaphat, the area that hooks along the Kidron Valley at the south end of Jerusalem. Half of the people in the city are destroyed or taken into captivity. The destruction and devastation are hard to imagine. The nation of Israel is battered, broken and beaten. She is nearly destroyed . . . but it's not over yet. In her darkest hour, when all seems lost, the nation will cry out to God for deliverance. And God will answer. This is the final phase of Armageddon.

> The Lord also will roar from Zion, and utter His voice from Jerusalem; the heavens and earth will shake; but the Lord will be a shelter for His people, and the strength of the children of Israel. "So you shall know that I am the Lord your God, dwelling in Zion My holy mountain. Then Jerusalem shall be holy, and no aliens shall ever pass through her again" (Joel 3:16,17).

You can read about the details of that deliverance in the next chapter. But remember, the battle of Armageddon will be the climax of a spiritual battle that has been going on since the beginning of time, a battle which is going on even now. While that war is ultimately between God and his adversary, Satan, the battle involves you and your choice either to turn to God and trust him, or to turn away and tune him out of your life.

It is the battle for the minds and hearts of men and women that is really the mother of all wars. It may appear to some that God is losing the battle, but he has shown through his prophets that he will allow those losses to go only so far before he claims the ultimate victory. God is not asleep at the wheel. What about you?

Maybe you haven't exactly been fighting God; you have only been trying to ignore him. Either way, you need to know that the battle lines have been drawn. God wants you to stand with him. There is no such thing as neutrality when it comes to this cosmic conflict; no spiritual Switzerland. Not choosing is a decision not to stand with God. Not only that, one day that decision will actually result in the non-chooser standing against God. God sent Messiah Y'shua to win the battle against sin and Satan so that you can share in the victory now. If you are willing to say "yes," if you choose to invite his rightful rule into your life, you can begin to experience the peace and hope he alone can bring. Turn to page 129 for help in joining God's side.

CHAPTER EIGHT

OUR GREAT HOPE

What is the Second Coming of Messiah?

"Then the sign of the Son of Man will appear in heaven, and then all the tribes of the earth will mourn, and they will see the Son of Man coming on the clouds of heaven with power and great glory" (Matthew 24:30).

In a scene from *Fiddler on the Roof,* the Jews of Anatevka have just been told they must leave their village. One villager asks the rabbi, "Rabbi, for so long we have waited for Messiah. Wouldn't this be a good time for him to come?" The rabbi responds, "We will just have to wait for him somewhere else."

Jewish people have hoped and longed for the Messiah throughout the ages. That hope is expressed daily in the synagogue prayer service: "Let the shoot of thy servant David sprout up quickly and raise up his horn with thy salvation, for all day long we hope for thy succor. . . ." It is also echoed in Maimonides' Thirteen Articles of Faith: "I believe with perfect faith in the coming of the Messiah and even though He tarry, nevertheless, I await Him every day that He should come."

But what will his coming bring? What will it be like? The following poem from the Middle Ages reflects the sense of ambiguity that many Jews feel about the coming of the Messiah:

Hurry, Messiah of God. Why do you tarry? Behold, they wait for you with flowing tears. Their tears of blood are like mighty streams. For you, O Prince, yearns every heart and tongue . . . Awake, our Messiah. Arise and shine. Mount a galloping horse, hitch up a royal carriage. Woe, all my bones are broken and are scattered. But should you ride an ass, my Lord, here's my advice: Go back to sleep, our Prince, and calm your heart. Let the end wait and the vision be sealed. (Raphael Patai, *The Messiah Texts,* New York: Avon Books, 1979, 49.)

Can you see how anxious longing for Messiah is tempered by some uncertainty as to how he will come and what he will do? We, as a people have a history of getting caught up in severe conflicts concerning the Messiah. In the Middle Ages, many pretenders claimed to be the Messiah—and many of our people followed them, with tragic results.

The rabbis concluded early on that the Jewish people ought not to make determinations about the Messiah's coming. "Cursed be they who calculate the end, because they argue that since the end has arrived, and the Messiah has not come, he will never come" (Sanhedrin 97*b*).

In other words, if people invest themselves in speculating about the Messiah and their theories do not prove true, they may become cynical about his coming. That cynicism may even lead others astray.

Here is the tension many of our people feel about the coming of the Messiah: on the one hand there is a tradition of longing, of deep, profound hope that the Messiah will come—while on the other hand there is great reticence to think in terms of specific dates or other particulars concerning the Messiah.

PUZZLING PORTRAITS OF MESSIAH

Perhaps another part of this ambivalence stems from a seeming ambiguity in the Bible itself. There appear to be two very different pictures of what the Messiah will be like.

The following passages compare these two pictures to highlight the apparent contradictions:

1) Daniel 7:14 and Daniel 9:26

> Then to Him was given dominion and glory and a kingdom, that all peoples, nations, and languages should serve Him. His dominion is an everlasting dominion, which shall not pass away, and His kingdom the one which shall not be destroyed (Daniel 7:14).

> And after the sixty-two weeks Messiah shall be cut off, but not for Himself; and the people of the prince who is to come shall destroy the city and the sanctuary. The end of it shall be with a flood, and till the end of the war desolations are determined (Daniel 9:26).

How can both be true? Daniel prophesies that the Messiah will have a glorious kingdom in which he will rule forever. It seems reasonable to assume that a forever ruler would be immortal. Yet a mere two chapters later, Daniel says that the Messiah will die and that the city and Temple will be destroyed.

2) Isaiah 9:6,7 and Isaiah 53:1-6

> For unto us a Child is born, unto us a Son is given; and the government will be upon His shoulder. And His name will be called Wonderful, Counselor, Mighty God, Everlasting Father, Prince of Peace. Of the increase of His government and peace there will be no end, upon the throne of David and over His kingdom, to order it and

establish it with judgment and justice from that time forward, even forever. The zeal of the LORD of hosts will perform this (Isaiah 9:6,7).

Who has believed our report? And to whom has the arm of the LORD been revealed? For He shall grow up before Him as a tender plant, and as a root out of dry ground. He has no form or comeliness; and when we see Him, there is no beauty that we should desire Him. He is despised and rejected by men, a Man of sorrows and acquainted with grief. And we hid, as it were, our faces from Him; He was despised, and we did not esteem Him. Surely He has borne our griefs and carried our sorrows; yet we esteemed Him stricken, smitten by God, and afflicted. But He was wounded for our transgressions, He was bruised for our iniquities; the chastisement for our peace was upon Him, and by His stripes we are healed. All we like sheep have gone astray; we have turned, every one, to his own way; and the LORD has laid on Him the iniquity of us all (Isaiah 53:1-6).

These passages offer one of the most striking of all the messianic contrasts. First the prophecy of the birth of a special child on whose shoulders the government rests. This child's extraordinary nature will be reflected in the exalted names by which people will call him, names that speak of the very character and qualities of God. Then once again, the very same prophet paints a portrait of one who is not accorded any honor, who in fact is rejected by those he came to heal. This is a humble servant who suffers for the sins of the nation and who eventually dies.

3) Daniel 7:13 and Zechariah 9:9

I was watching in the night visions, and behold, One like the Son of Man, coming with the clouds of Heaven! He came to the Ancient of Days, and they brought Him near before Him (Daniel 7:13).

Rejoice greatly, O daughter of Zion! Shout, O daughter of Jerusalem! Behold, your King is coming to you; He is just and having salvation, lowly and riding on a donkey, a colt, the foal of a donkey (Zechariah 9:9).

Here are two more pictures of the Messiah, this time with very different means of transport: one shows him coming in the clouds of Heaven, the other on the foal of a donkey. So which is it?

In each case, we have these two very different pictures of the Messiah. What is the solution?

POSSIBLE SOLUTIONS TO THE PUZZLE

Jewish tradition offers two interesting solutions to the puzzling portraits of Messiah, and the *Brit Ha Chadasha,* the New Testament offers another. Let's compare them.

According to one Jewish tradition, there are actually two messiahs to come: Messiah son of Joseph and Messiah son of David:

"And the land shall mourn," Zechariah 12:12, what is the reason of this mourning? Rabbi Docce says, "They will mourn over the Messiah who will be slain . . . the Holy One, Blessed be He will say to Messiah Ben David, 'May He be revealed soon in our days. Ask of me anything and I shall give it to you. . . .' And when he will see that Messiah Ben Joseph will be slain he will say before him, 'Master of the world, I ask nothing of you except life.' God will say to him, 'Even before you said life, your father David prophesied about you as it is written, "He asked life of thee, thou gavest it him"'" (Sukkot 52*a*).

The talmudic passage above depicts a dialogue between Messiah Son of David and the LORD God himself. God offers the Messiah Son of David anything he wants, and his request is this: that when Messiah Son of Joseph dies, God should raise him back to life. God replies that it had already been prophesied that Messiah son of David would make that very request ... and that God would indeed grant it.

Another Jewish tradition explains the two contrasting portraits of Messiah in the following way: "Rabbi Alexandri said, 'Rabbi Y'hoshu ben Levi explained, "If the people of Israel will be righteous, the Messiah will come in the clouds of Heaven. If they will not be righteous, he will come as a poor man riding upon an ass"'" (Sanhedrin 98*a*).

This second explanation suggests that the manner in which the Messiah is coming (in the clouds of Heaven or on a donkey) will be determined by whether or not Israel is righteous.

TWO PORTRAITS, TWO COMINGS, ONE MESSIAH

The New Testament presents a very different view of the seemingly divergent prophecies. It is an earlier Jewish view, albeit a minority view. (Remember, the New Testament was written by first century Jewish believers in Jesus, whereas much of the Talmud was written between the second and fifth centuries A.D.). The New Testament view is that the contrasting prophecies describe one Messiah who will come twice.

> Of this salvation the prophets have inquired and searched carefully, who prophesied of the grace that would come to you, searching what, or what manner of time, the Spirit of Christ [Messiah] who was in them was indicating when He testified beforehand the sufferings of Christ and the glories that would follow (1 Peter 1:10,11).

Peter pointed out that when you look at the prophecies concerning the coming of Messiah, you see both the sufferings and the glories to follow. Same Messiah, different experiences. Think of it as a distant view of two mountains. From far away, the mountains appear to be right next to each other, perhaps even touching. But as you travel the long distance to approach the first mountain, and you begin the upward ascent, the large distance between the two mountains becomes more and more apparent. This is often the case with prophecy. The prophets saw the two pictures of the Messiah as two mountains. They appear to be on the same plane, perhaps even touching, but they are actually separated by a wide time span. According to this New Testament perspective, the Messiah came once as a suffering servant to atone for the sins of the people. He will come again in power and glory to bring everlasting justice and righteousness.

Jesus was predicting his own return, when he confidently promised his followers: "And if I go and prepare a place for you I will come back and take you to be with me that you also may be where I am."

After his crucifixion and resurrection Jesus explained that both his suffering and his glory had been predicted by the Hebrew prophets:

> Then He said to them, "O foolish ones, and slow of heart to believe in all that the prophets have spoken! Ought not the Christ to have suffered these things and to enter into His glory?" And beginning at Moses and all the Prophets, He expounded to them in all the Scriptures the things concerning Himself (Luke 24:25-27).

Later, the author of the New Testament book of Hebrews expressed this same view in writing to Jesus' first century Jewish followers:

> ... so Christ was offered once to bear the sins of many. To those who eagerly wait for Him He will appear a second time, apart from sin, for salvation (Hebrews 9:28).

The New Testament solution is not two messiahs, but two comings of the same Messiah. It is that second coming that his followers are awaiting, and which plays into the end times scenario.

HOW WILL IT HAPPEN?

To see it in context, let's recap the scenario presented from previous chapters. The world has reached a paroxysm of military conflict. Seven years of tribulation have come to a roaring crescendo of bloodshed and violence. All of the nations of the earth have gathered to fight against Israel. The blood of Jews and Gentiles and the stench of death has filled the valley of Jehoshaphat. The furious screams of the dying fill the ears of all those gathered in this ancient land. A lethal dagger is poised at the heart of the Jewish people, ready for the kill. God, who promised that Israel would be his people forever, is their only hope. At this point all of Israel cries out in the agony of a people who have come to the very end of themselves. There is nowhere left to turn. The hour is upon them. Hope is nearly gone.

It is then that the Messiah comes in power and in glory. The Bible gives us the sequence. The first thing you notice is the sound of his coming; you hear it before you see him. The sights, sounds and the smell of battle have been all-intrusive until that point, but they all fade out of focus as the overwhelming, overpowering sound of the coming King fills the air and "the Lord Himself descends with a shout" (1 Thessalonians 4:16).

What must the shout of the Creator of the Universe sound like? I imagine that it begins not in the ears, but in the bones. It reverberates throughout the body, and beyond, through the valleys and over the mountain tops. The rocks and the ground are trembling at the sound of his voice. All people, in fact all creatures, stop short in rapt attention. That sound is then joined by another powerful sound, "the voice of the archangel."

What does an archangel sound like? It is certainly otherworldly, not like any earthly being or musical instrument. I imagine it is a forceful sound that weaves itself around the already overpowering shout of the Messiah. Is it beautiful? Melodious? We don't know. Then comes the third and final sound, "the trumpet call of God." This is not the brass instrument of a marching band or orchestra. It is the ancient call of the ram's horn, the shofar, in all its eerie and penetrating holiness.

The Messiah, the archangel, the shofar of God. This heavenly trio brings all sound, indeed all activity on planet Earth to a halt. All creatures, man and beast, become still as their eyes are drawn inexorably skyward. Imagine you are there. What do you see? The dark clouds of conflict have been cleared. The Light—brighter, clearer and more brilliant than anything ever seen—bursts not merely into sight, but into your very soul. Myriads of angels as well as people fill the sky, but all eyes are fixed on that great hope, the Messiah.

> I saw heaven standing open and there before me was a white horse, whose rider is called Faithful and True. With justice he judges and makes war. His eyes are like blazing fire, and on his head are many crowns. He has a name written on him that no one knows but he himself. He is dressed in a robe dipped in blood, and his name is the Word of God. The armies of heaven were following him, riding on white horses and dressed in fine linen, white and clean. Out of his mouth comes a sharp sword with which to strike down the nations. "He will rule them with an iron scepter." He treads the wine press of the fury of the wrath of God Almighty. On his robe and on his thigh he has this name written: KING OF KINGS AND LORD OF LORDS (Revelation 19:11-16).

Such a vision with all the blinding light of Heaven's glory will do more than put a pause in the conflict on earth, it will instantly accomplish the greatest military victory in human history. Zechariah describes the weapon of God as something like a thermonuclear warhead, yet it only affects those who are the armies of the Antichrist.

> And this shall be the plague with which the LORD will strike all the people who fought against Jerusalem: their flesh shall dissolve while they stand on their feet,

their eyes shall dissolve in their sockets, and their
tongues shall dissolve in their mouths. It shall come to
pass in that day that a great panic from the LORD will be
among them. Everyone will seize the hand of his
neighbor, and raise his hand against his neighbor's hand
(Zechariah 14:12,13).

The war will be over before Messiah ever reaches the earth.
While he is still descending from the clouds all of Israel's
attackers will be vanquished in a single instant. And as the foot
of Messiah touches down upon this planet, the very topography
of the Middle East is altered. As he descends onto the Mount of
Olives east of the city of Jerusalem, the mere touch of his foot
causes that mountain to split in two.

All that transpires is supernatural, almost beyond human
comprehension. The desert region to the east and south
known as the Dead Sea region is instantaneously transformed
into a garden with rivers and flowers and wildlife. The very
presence of Messiah begins to transform this tortured, war-torn
world into a place of peace and tranquillity. But it is not just
the planet that is changed. The people are transformed as well.
Israel, so long in unbelief, now recognizes her Messiah:

And I will pour on the house of David and on the
inhabitants of Jerusalem the Spirit of grace and supplication;
then they will look on Me whom they have pierced; they
will mourn for Him as one mourns for his only son, and
grieve for Him as one grieves for a firstborn. . . . In that day
a fountain shall be opened for the house of David and for
the inhabitants of Jerusalem, for sin and for uncleanness
(Zechariah 12:10; 13:1).

He is the pierced one. His name is Y'shua. Jesus. The one
whose birth and death mark the time by which human history
has been measured. The nation of Israel has turned away from
Y'shua for 2000 years. But when he comes back, there will be

no more turning away. The whole world will acknowledge him as the King of Israel and the Savior of the world. He will bring together Jews and Gentiles into his kingdom on the earth. (More about that in the next chapter.)

The returning Messiah is our great Hope. He is the dawn that comes after the darkest hour. But his way was paved with suffering. The one who will come on the clouds in power and glory first had to come on the foal of a donkey. The one who will judge the earth first had to die as a sacrifice for sin. And the world will also undergo great suffering before he returns to rescue the remnant of those not lost in the mother of all wars.

Those who are now "in between" the time of the Messiah's first and second coming have a decision to make and an opportunity to take. Jesus has been transforming lives all along, rescuing those who are able to see that they need God's forgiveness, redeeming those who recognize the sacrifice he made to atone for our sin. There is no need to wait for the mountain to be split in two. The Messiah is close at hand, only a prayer away from transforming your life today and forever. Turn to page 129 to receive his love and forgiveness now.

CHAPTER NINE

MAY YOUR KINGDOM COME

What does the Bible say about the messianic age?

"And the Lord shall be King over all the earth. In that day it shall be—'The Lord is one,' and His name one" (Zechariah 14:9).

People have an interesting way of using their automobiles to express their hopes and dreams, among other things. One popular bumper sticker reads, "Visualize World Peace." Another, less popular, sticker counters, "Visualize Whirled Peas," in a cynical play on the notion that we can somehow, by the force of our will, bring something as enormous yet illusive as world peace into existence.

Deep in the heart of every human being is an abiding awareness that things are not the way they should be. Many still hold on to the hope that some day, somehow, things will change. Peace will come. It may seem idealistic at best to think that people can create peace simply by wanting it and thinking about it, but there is One whose will is sufficient to make peace a reality. God. And he has promised to do it.

Imagine that all your best, most noble wishes for the way the world should be could come true: justice for all people, no more hunger or homelessness or crime. Imagine all the evil in the world replaced by a universal commitment to do right, to respect one another. Imagine a flourishing of creativity in which there would be whole new levels of music, art and poetry. What you are imagining has been called various things: utopia, nirvana, the best of all possible worlds, heaven on earth. The Bible calls it the Kingdom of God. It is the morning of The Day of the Lord.

Some people believe that when the Messiah returns he will immediately usher us all into eternity. I am convinced that he will first establish the Kingdom of God on this earth, a kingdom in which the whole world will experience one thousand years of his peaceful rule. This thousand-year rule of Messiah on the earth is commonly called "the Millennium."

PROMISES FULFILLED, HOPE JUSTIFIED

The Millennium contains some special provisions for Israel. You see, God made some promises to the Jewish people that have yet to be fulfilled, and part of his purpose in this reign will be to keep those promises. For example:

On the same day the LORD made a covenant with Abram, saying: "To your descendants I have given this land, from the river of Egypt to the great river, the River Euphrates" (Genesis 15:18).

The land God promised had very specific boundaries; from the Euphrates River to what is called the River of Egypt. The river of Egypt is not the Nile. It is a stream or wadi that runs down through the middle of the Sinai peninsula. Israel has never fully possessed that territory. God promised the Land to Abram and his descendants, and God always keeps his promises. The prophets look forward to a time when that promise will be fulfilled and so can we (see Isaiah 27:12).

God also made a promise to David—to establish his throne forever.

I have made a covenant with My chosen, I have sworn to My servant David: "Your seed I will establish forever, and build up your throne to all generations." . . . Once I have sworn by My holiness; I will not lie to David: his seed shall endure forever, and his throne as the sun before Me; it shall be established forever like the moon, even like the faithful witness in the sky (Psalm 89:3,4,35-37).

Only the Messiah, who is the descendant of David, can fulfill that promise. The prophets looked forward to a restoration of David's throne on the earth:

On that day I will raise up the tabernacle of David, which has fallen down, and repair its damages; I will raise up its ruins, and rebuild it as in the days of old . . . (Amos 9:11).

Finally, we have promises concerning a new covenant God said he would make with Israel:

Behold, the days are coming, says the LORD, when I will make a new covenant with the house of Israel and with the house of Judah—not according to the covenant that I made with their fathers in the day that I took them by the hand to lead them out of the land of Egypt, My covenant which they broke, though I was a husband to them, says the Lord. But this is the covenant that I will make with the house of Israel after those days, says the Lord: I will put My law in their minds, and write it on their hearts; and I will be their God, and they shall be My people. No more shall every man teach his neighbor, and every man his brother, saying, "Know the Lord," for they all shall know Me, from the least of them to the greatest of them, says the Lord. For I will forgive

their iniquity, and their sin I will remember no more
(Jeremiah 31:31-34).

Those of us who believe that Jesus is the Messiah believe that
this new covenant has been established; he has kept this promise
to us as individuals. Nevertheless the full expression of that new
covenant will not be realized until all people know the Lord.
The prophet Habakkuk paints a wonderful picture of this
amazing phenomenon:

> For the earth will be filled with the knowledge of the glory
> of the Lord, as the waters cover the sea (Habakkuk 2:14).

KINGDOM JUSTICE: AN END TO FEAR
Another purpose that the Messiah will fulfill during his
thousand-year reign on earth will be to demonstrate perfect
justice.

> His delight is in the fear of the LORD, and He shall not judge
> by the sight of His eyes, nor decide by the hearing of His
> ears; but with righteousness He shall judge the poor, and
> decide with equity for the meek of the earth; He shall
> strike the earth with the rod of His mouth, and with the
> breath of His lips He shall slay the wicked (Isaiah 11:3,4).

Again, take a moment to imagine how this will change
everything. All of humanity longs for justice. These days, when
people face legal problems they hire a lawyer. Then they go to
court and hope their lawyer is better than their opponent's,
and that he or she can persuade the judge to rule in their favor.
The Messiah is going to transform the legal system. In the
Kingdom, people will go to the judge to find out what is right,
not to find out if he'll side with them. His justice will be perfect
and righteous. How often do people say, "That's not fair"? That
phrase will disappear from our vocabulary. Our coming King
will apply righteous justice evenly and swiftly.

And what about an end to crime? Man's inhumanity to man plays itself out every day in the major (and not so major) cities of this world. Robbery, rape and murder are all common occurrences and all too many people live in fear. How often do our fears drive us? You are walking down a dark street and you hear footsteps behind you. You find that knot in your stomach. Fear. Your child is playing at a neighbor's house down the street and doesn't return home on time. You call the neighbor's house and there is a note of concern, an edge of panic, in your voice.

In the Kingdom there will be no more cause for fear. Even the little indignities of life that cause us to be fearful will disappear because Messiah will bring a perfect peace.

But everyone shall sit under his vine and under his fig tree, and no one shall make them afraid; for the mouth of the LORD of hosts has spoken (Micah 4:4).

A WORLD OF CHANGE

And it won't just be the social order that is transformed. The earth will be like the Garden of Eden once was. Nature itself will be restored. There won't be a need for an Environmental Protection Agency or a Greenpeace. The enmity between humans and animals—even between the animals themselves—will be abolished.

The wolf also shall dwell with the lamb, the leopard shall lie down with the young goat, the calf and the young lion and the fatling together; and a little child shall lead them. The cow and the bear shall graze; their young ones shall lie down together; and the lion shall eat straw like the ox. The nursing child shall play by the cobra's hole, and the weaned child shall put his hand in the viper's den (Isaiah 11:6-8).

Moreover, the Messiah will eradicate tragedy and fear. Have you ever had to sit by and watch a loved one endure the ravages of a killer disease such as cancer? Or worse yet, see a young person's life end before even reaching adulthood? Such suffering and grief will be banished from the Kingdom of God as the prophet Isaiah predicted:

> Never again will there be in it an infant that lives but a few days, or an old man who does not live out his years; he who dies at a hundred will be thought a mere youth; he who fails to reach a hundred will be considered accursed (Isaiah 65:20).

The spiritual order will also be transformed in the Millennium. Religion will no longer be a matter of opinion. Today proponents of a host of religions vie for people's minds and hearts. Even adherents of the same religion disagree among themselves on a whole range of theological issues. But when Y'shua returns, all such debates will cease. There will be no more wondering or arguing over who is right or who is wrong. We will all know the truth fully.

> They shall not hurt nor destroy in all My holy mountain, for the earth shall be full of the knowledge of the Lord as the waters cover the sea (Isaiah 11:9).

This knowledge will be expressed in an amazing and unified system of worship centered in Jerusalem—in a brand new Temple. The prophet Ezekiel describes this astonishing place of worship in chapters 40-48. In many ways it will be similar to the previous Temples in Jerusalem: it will have an outer court, an inner court, a porch, a holy place and a most holy place. It will have paneled wood, palm trees and cherubim as in the previous temples. However, in the most holy place there will be no ark, no mercy seat, no veil, no high priest—only the table of shew bread. There will be other startling differences. The Temple itself will be huge, fully one square mile. Within that Temple, there will be a throne, and of all things, a river. That river will flow out of the Temple all the way down to the Dead

Sea. And it will make the Dead Sea alive!

The presence of a throne in this Temple is most significant. It indicates a theocratic form of government, meaning government run by God. Our U.S. society is very concerned about maintaining "separation between church and state." The fear of mixing the two stems from a history of religious persecution; when government has been guided by religion, those who do not adhere to the dominant religion have typically suffered. Such concerns will be unwarranted in the Kingdom of God. There will be no minority religions because everyone will be worshiping the one true God!

What may be difficult for people in our society to grasp is that freedom of religion will be irrelevant when the Messiah comes to reign and to rule, just as the concept of democracy will be irrelevant.

This may sound frightening to some, but only because we have lost sight of the true purposes of religion and government, and the meaning of freedom.

The purpose of religion is not to express our individuality or our preferences, although many people today have used religion to do just that. Many think in terms of choosing a religion that best expresses their personality and/or values. But the real function of religion is to provide a vehicle through which we can relate to God. The way to have a relationship with God is to discover and accept the truth about what he wants and expects of us.

Likewise, the purpose of government is not to allow the people of a sovereign state to administrate their opinions of what is acceptable or not acceptable in their society. We in the United States believe that democracy is the best possible way for imperfect people to hold one another accountable for what is right. We rejected monarchy because we believed that absolute power corrupts absolutely.

Such reasoning will not apply in the kingdom, because the One who wields absolute power there is incorruptible. Y'shua, God incarnate, has every right to rule. And he is also the rightful object of worship. The one who sits on the throne in the Temple is the one who rules over all the nations. All the peoples of the world will recognize that this is his mandated place. The global freedom that they will experience is the freedom to come before the Holy One of Israel, the liberty to be loyal subjects of a wise and loving King who is always just and true.

This Temple is not just for the Jewish people. It is the place of worship for all the nations of the world.

Now it shall come to pass in the latter days that the mountain of the Lord's house shall be established on the top of the mountains, and shall be exalted above the hills; and all nations shall flow to it. Many people shall come and say, "Come, and let us go up to the mountain of the Lord, to the house of the God of Jacob; He will teach us His ways, and we shall walk in His paths." For out of Zion shall go forth the law, and the word of the Lord from Jerusalem (Isaiah 2:2,3).

ISRAEL'S DESTINY
The millennial Temple will bring the final and complete fulfillment of God's promise that, through Abraham, all the nations of the earth will be blessed. Jesus looked forward to this day when he first walked the earth. He said of the future Temple in Jerusalem, "For my house shall be called a house of prayer for all the nations" (Matthew 21:13).

The Bible clearly indicates that Israel is God's chosen people, the apple of his eye—his special one. People struggle with that, even Jewish people seem afraid to embrace the concept; it seems so ethnocentric, so nonegalitarian, so arrogant. Why should Israel be regarded as special? It's helpful for Jews and Gentiles to read what the Bible has to say about this "chosenness." In so doing, both can accept Israel's destiny with a sense of humility.

The Bible points out that God never chose Israel because we were such a great people, but because the God of Israel is a great God, a God who chose for his own reasons to use a small and seemingly insignificant people to be his light to the world. He made specific promises to Abraham, Isaac and Jacob and while the focus of his promises may seem narrow, the results were always intended to be universal. ("In you all the families of the earth will be blessed.")

In the Kingdom of God, the blessings of Israel will become a shared blessing with all of the nations of the world. God will actually restore the fortunes, not only of Jacob, but of the *goyim,* the nations. One of the greatest examples of that is God's promise to take two nations that historically have been Israel's arch enemies, and elevate them to the status of blessedness with Israel.

In that day there will be a highway from Egypt to Assyria, and the Assyrian will come into Egypt and the Egyptian into Assyria, and the Egyptians will serve with the Assyrians (Isaiah 19:23).

What a powerful vision. These warring nations will actually share equally in the blessings of God. Visualize World Peace? The Bible has. It is called the Kingdom of God and it will be beautiful beyond words. If you understand the vision of what is to come then you will understand the significance of what Y'shua meant when he taught his followers to pray, "Your Kingdom come, Your will be done on earth as it is in heaven" (Matthew 6:10).

The good news is that you don't have to wait to begin experiencing the Kingdom of God. The Kingdom of God begins in the heart and becomes rooted in each person who acknowledges Jesus as King. God is bringing Jews and Gentiles, people of every tribe and tongue and nation together under his rule right now. You can receive him as your king today. You will not yet experience Heaven on earth in the sense of being in a world where everyone is living under God's righteous rule—but you will begin to experience Heaven in your heart as God starts his transformation process. You can know his peace and forgiveness, and he will guide you and show you how to live without fear in the midst of a world that is still rebelling against him. You can pray, too, for the Kingdom of God to begin in your heart right now. If you need help, turn to page 129.

CHAPTER TEN

THE REAL SUPREME COURT

Is there a final judgment?

"The LORD stands up to plead, and stands to judge the people" (Isaiah 3:13).

"How dare you judge me!" Most people have said it and/or heard it said to them. And even if we don't say anything out loud, which of us hasn't bristled when we feel someone is being judgmental toward us? In our postmodern world, telling people they are "judgmental" is just about the worst insult you can level at them.

Judgment. The very word conjures up bad images, uncomfortable feelings. We want to avoid being judged and we don't want others to think that we are judging them. Yet all of us pronounce judgments from childhood on through the course of our lives. "But you promised!" "Hey, why don't you wait in line like everyone else?" "You're not being fair." "Leave him alone, he isn't doing any harm." Each of those statements assumes some standard by which we can, perhaps even should, evaluate people's actions and attitudes.

103

IS EVERYTHING RELATIVE?

Many people say that standards of right and wrong are subjective and not applicable to all people and cultures, i.e., "My truth may not be your truth." Is it all relative? Certainly there are cultural morés that vary from one society to the next, morés that are so binding upon the people of a particular culture that they mistakenly see them as universal truths. However, the fact that there are relative standards does not mean that all standards are relative. Many people insist on the relative nature of right and wrong, but at our most basic level, we all know better.

What society would admire and promote cowardice, or find it laudable for family members and friends to betray one another's trust? Every society will recognize that certain things are right and others are wrong. That isn't to say that right and wrong are limited to or determined by the lowest common denominator between cultures. Still, the fact that there is such a denominator points out that people do have what some have described as an inner sense of "oughtness." What is the source of this inner sense?

Some say it is merely instinct. We learn to value certain standards as a matter of self-preservation. Some would add that we have an unspoken contract with other people in our community. A sense of "right" behavior is necessary to preserve society, and because we live in relation to others, our instincts to preserve society are really instincts to protect ourselves.

But is "oughtness" really a matter of self-preservation? Imagine yourself in a boat in the middle of a storm. You see a drowning man not far from you. The water is swirling all around and you know that if you jump in, you may well die. Your sense of self-preservation screams at you, "Stay in the boat!" But what else do you feel? You feel that you SHOULD help the drowning man. No one is there to place expectations on you or blame you if you stay in the boat. Yet you can't help feeling you ought do the exact opposite of that which is in your own interest. Isn't that strange?

We do have a sense of oughtness, standards of right and wrong that we know innately, and by which we judge ourselves and others. Those inner tuggings about right and wrong point to the One who is the standard for all that is right and the judge of all that is wrong: the Creator—the God of the Bible. God is the source of morality, which is why he designed us with that sense of oughtness. And considering that God is the most powerful being in the universe, aren't you really glad that he has standards of right and wrong?

When we say that we don't want to be judged, it isn't that we don't care to see principles of right and wrong upheld. What we usually mean is that we don't believe in someone else's right to say that we are wrong.

JUDGMENT: WHO NEEDS IT?

We sense, when people judge us, that they are somehow elevating themselves at our expense. We may find it difficult to ignore other people's shortcomings, yet we feel mistreated if anyone should evaluate our actions, much less attitudes, and find them lacking. We dislike hypocrisy in others but tend to explain away our own "inconsistencies." We all very much want to be right.

It's not a bad thing to want to be right. We were created in God's image and maybe that is why we have such a hunger to see ourselves as good. The problem is, we tend to finagle and mess with standards of right and wrong rather than admit (even to ourselves) that we don't measure up to them. Some of the attitudes and actions that we accept in ourselves fall pretty short of God's standards. That is what the Bible means when it talks about sin. Sin is not simply a matter of committing an act that is unacceptable by societal standards; it's not even a matter of violating our own principles. Sin is a matter of missing God's standards. Sometimes it is a matter of declaring our independence from God, and saying that we don't need his standards or his approval. Sometimes sin is a matter of presuming or even insisting that God approves of our standards, without ever trying to find out if he does . . . and without any willingness to know if he doesn't.

WHAT IS A HOLY GOD TO DO?

Unlike some people, God does not delight in judging us. He has no need to be elevated by putting others down—after all, God is elevated above all and he has a perfect self-image. He does not judge from a desire to look down on us; he loves us and truly wants us to be righteous and blameless. Unfortunately, we simply don't measure up—and God can't treat our sin like it doesn't matter. To do so would violate his righteousness and holiness. That righteousness, that holiness requires God to right the wrongs, to punish those who do evil, to administer justice.

Many people have wondered how a God of love could pour out the kind of judgment, even wrath, that we see throughout the Bible. In thinking it through, we might just as well ask how a loving God could *not* pour out wrath. Our court systems, imperfect as they are, daily determine what is right and wrong and dole out punishment. We all recognize the need for justice in society. Is God less able to determine right and wrong than our courts? Is he less concerned with justice than you or I?

Part of God's loving nature is his willingness to exercise true judgment and establish real justice. Evil cries out for judgment. Look at the atrocities committed all over the world, listen to the news each day. People are inflicting horrible suffering on one another, and victims include even the most vulnerable in our society—children. Your innermost being cries out and screams, "This has to stop—those people have to pay for what they have done." And they will. Because as ugly and vile as such excesses and abuses appear to us, how much more so to a holy and just God?

Some people feel that all the evil in the world is proof that either God does not exist, or that he can't do much to bring justice. Yet the very fact that we know evil for what it is points to the existence of a good and righteous God, who has made us with some understanding of the way things should be. And God does bring justice; sometimes it is swift and sometimes it is delayed.

Throughout Jewish tradition we see evidence of the belief in a God who judges and in the fact that ultimate judgment comes when we reach the end of our lives. The Hebrew service for a funeral begins with the blessing: *"Baruch Atah Adonai, Elohenu Melech HaOlam Dayan Ha Emet. . . ."* "Blessed are You Lord our God, King of the Universe, the True Judge." The author of the New Testament book of Hebrews put it another way: "And as it is appointed for men to die once, but after this the judgment" (Hebrews 9:27). Or to put it another way, it may be easy to merely mouth the words when performing in the choir of life, but someday that performance will end and each of us will have to sing a solo before God.

So God not only has a right, but an obligation, to judge. He always gives fair warning, though, regarding his judgments and he patiently provides us with an alternative—up to a point.

HERE COMES THE JUDGE

The Bible describes two types of judgments. The first are known as temporal judgments, those that take place in time and space and serve a purpose confined to the present. The second are final judgments, those acts of God with enduring consequences. In other words, they are eternal and unchanging judgments. The Bible, in describing the end of the world, mentions both types of judgment. The temporal judgments are the catastrophic events that will befall the world during the Great Tribulation. After that, the final judgments, also known as Throne Judgments, will usher us into eternity.

Many think of judgment as purely punitive. While it is true that God judges to punish evil, that is not the main reason for judgment. God's judgment reveals and establishes God's character. God's moral perfection, righteousness, justice, wisdom, omniscience, omnipotence—all these things cry out against the injustice, the unrighteousness, the foolishness and depravity we see all around us. God must judge these things because his character requires it. God's judgment establishes who he is before the earth and for all eternity.

A second element of judgment is retribution, not only punishment, but reward as well. Without punishment for evil, reward for righteousness is a mockery. Without rewards for righteousness, punishment for evil is tyrannical. God's judgment takes into account both the evil and the good. God is not capricious. He is not arbitrary. He consistently applies a perfect standard, his own character, as he judges the behavior and heart attitudes of humans in this world.

The Bible's descriptions of the temporal judgments during the Great Tribulation can be likened to scenes on a mural illustrating a huge battle. The battle is ultimately between God and Satan, but the warfare is conducted on the earth and among humans. One of the keys to understanding these judgments is that the Bible shows them from God's perspective. The Bible describes various people and events in ways that enable us to see their true nature. For example, the Bible depicts the Antichrist as the Beast. That is his character from God's perspective: a beast coming out of the depths. But how will he be seen from a human standpoint? He will be accepted and even worshiped. From a human perspective, the Antichrist is a highly charismatic figure, a wise and worldly leader. But God warns us with a biblical perspective that shows what he really is. That is typical of how the Bible depicts all of the end time judgments.

In another example, the Bible describes locusts that come up out of the deep, horrible monster-like creatures with hair and teeth, like nothing ever seen before. These locusts cannot take people's lives, but when they attack they inflict such suffering that people want to die. Will we actually see such creatures afflicting people in the Tribulation? No we won't. They represent demonic beings that will be invisible to human eyes, but the devastation they bring will be very real.

Think of the book of Job, and how we see all his sufferings from an earthly perspective as well as from a spiritual perspective. All the catastrophes that befell Job seemed like natural disasters striking from out of the blue, but we are made privy, in the first chapter, to the fact that they are a result of a spiritual conflict. So it is with the end time judgments. The Bible unmasks the heavenly version of all these events.

TRIBULATION JUDGMENTS

The book of Revelation tells about three sets of judgments during the Great Tribulation: each set has a series of seven judgments. The judgments are known as the seven seals, the seven trumpets and the seven bowls. Most of these temporal judgments will come as natural disasters: famines, plagues, earthquakes, terrible war and disease. Many people will witness these judgments and cry out to God in repentance. But the majority of the world will blame God for their sufferings, rather than turning to him:

> And they blasphemed the God of Heaven because of their pains and their sores, and did not repent of their deeds (Revelation 16:11).

Just as the Bible predicts three sets of temporal judgments, so there will also be three separate and final judgments occurring at different points. The first is called the Judgment Seat of Messiah, the second is the Judgment of the Nations and the third is the Great White Throne Judgment.

THE JUDGMENT SEAT OF MESSIAH

The Judgment Seat of Messiah is the judgment of believers in Y'shua, and will occur following the Rapture, described in Chapter Three.

> For we must all appear before the judgment seat of Christ, that each one may receive the things done in the body, according to what he has done, whether good or bad (2 Corinthians 5:10).

Each person who has trusted in Y'shua as Messiah and Sin Bearer will spend eternity with him in Heaven, but within that category there are various levels of faithfulness. Those who did little to concern themselves with obedience to God while on the earth will be judged as lacking. They will have a place in Heaven but will receive no other reward. Those who have lived their lives faithfully for God will not only be with the Lord forever, they will enjoy rewards and blessings based on their faithfulness.

JUDGMENT OF THE NATIONS

The second judgment is the Judgment of the Nations. That will happen when the Messiah returns to save Israel at the end of the last battle.

> Let the nations be wakened, and come up to the Valley of Jehoshaphat; for there I will sit to judge all the surrounding nations. Put in the sickle, for the harvest is ripe. Come, go down; for the winepress is full, the vats overflow—for their wickedness is great. Multitudes, multitudes in the valley of decision. For the day of the LORD is near in the valley of decision. The sun and moon will grow dark, and the stars will diminish their brightness. The LORD also will roar from Zion, and utter His voice from Jerusalem; the heavens and earth will shake; but the LORD will be a shelter for His people, and the strength of the children of Israel (Joel 3:12-16).

The Judgment of the Nations happens at the very end of the Tribulation and it applies to those who are living on the earth at that time. Those who oppose the Messiah, who have aligned themselves with the Antichrist and against Israel, will be judged and delivered into "the abyss." They will be held there until the final judgment. Those who have accepted Y'shua as Messiah will become citizens of his kingdom. The result of this judgment is the establishment of the Kingdom of

God on the earth, the thousand-year reign described in Chapter Nine. That is the period of time when true judgment and justice will be established on the earth.

FINAL JUDGMENT: THE GREAT WHITE THRONE

The last of the final judgments is called the Great White Throne Judgment.

> Then I saw a great white throne and Him who sat on it, from whose face the earth and the heaven fled away. And there was found no place for them. And I saw the dead, small and great, standing before God, and books were opened. And another book was opened, which is the Book of Life. And the dead were judged according to their works, by the things which were written in the books. The sea gave up the dead who were in it, and Death and Hades delivered up the dead who were in them. And they were judged, each one according to his works. Then Death and Hades were cast into the lake of fire. This is the second death. And anyone not found written in the Book of Life was cast into the lake of fire (Revelation 20:11-15).

So, who does the writer say is judged at the Great White Throne Judgment? People who have died without having put their trust in Jesus are resurrected for final judgment. All of the people who are living during Messiah's Kingdom rule on the earth will also be judged. Satan, who had been bound during the Kingdom period and then was loosed at the very end, is also judged at this time. Finally, death and Hell itself are judged and sent into the lake of fire.

THE BOOK OF LIFE

The Bible tells us that there is a very simple test that is used as the basis for judgment at the Great White Throne. A heavenly ledger, called the Book of Life, will contain the names of those who need not fear judgment. Everyone else, should. This is not a new concept. At Rosh Hashanah many Jewish people greet one another with the phrase, *L'shana tova tikatevu,* "May your name be written for good year." It implies that if you are in this book, your well-being is secure. The prophet Daniel also speaks of this "book":

> At that time Michael shall stand up, the great prince who stands watch over the sons of your people; and there shall be a time of trouble, such as never was since there was a nation, even to that time. And at that time your people shall be delivered, every one who is found written in the book. And many of those who sleep in the dust of the earth shall awake, some to everlasting life, some to shame and everlasting contempt (Daniel 12:1,2).

It seems simple enough. Either your name is there or it is not, and your eternal destiny will be decided by that fact. But how does one get written into the Book of Life?

If we had to stand before God's judgment based on our goodness, none of our names would be written in his book because none of us are good enough to come into the presence of a perfect and holy God. But Jesus came to make an atonement, a covering for all of our sin. He did that by dying on the cross. God looked upon that act as payment for our sins and faults. Because our Messiah was the Holy One, the only Son of God, his perfect life and atoning death defeated sin and death and that is how and why he rose from the dead.

> Jesus said to her, "I am the resurrection and the life. He who believes in Me, though he may die, he shall live. And whoever lives and believes in Me shall never die . . ." (John 11:25,26).

If we stand before God, not trusting in our own righteousness, but in Y'shua's righteousness, we will be judged according to his righteousness. Our sins were already judged and paid for when he died for us. If we believe and receive that gift, we won't experience this "second death" of God's judgment, but will live forever with him.

Interested? The only catch is that offer of eternal life is limited—you must decide during this lifetime. If you have, you can be certain that your name is written in the Book of Life and you can be assured of your entrance into the very presence of the Creator of the Universe. If you are not certain how to accept this gift, turn to page 129.

CHAPTER ELEVEN

ETERNITY

What about Heaven and Hell?

*"He has made everything beautiful in its time. Also He has
put eternity in their hearts, except that no one can find out
the work that God does from beginning to end"
(Ecclesiastes 3:11).*

Imagine yourself in a South American rain forest, talking to
a man who has lived there all his life. He has had no
contact with the outside world, does not know what
electricity is and you are the first person he has met outside
of his own small community. Your task is to explain the
Internet to him.

Even if you have a perfect understanding of the complexities
of modern technology, that man has no frame of reference for
what you want to communicate. Unless you can take him out of
the rain forest and show him a whole world beyond his present
experience, he has as much chance of grasping your explanation
as a fish has of understanding a life outside of water.

The same is true of eternity. There is life beyond this present
realm we occupy. Though skeptics deny it, most people sense
that death is not the end of all things, but rather a portal to
something beyond. As the writer of Ecclesiastes put it, "God
has put eternity in our hearts." Most of us have pondered what
will happen after we die. What is Heaven like? Is there such a
place as Hell? The Bible speaks clearly and unequivocally about

the existence of both. We might wish that we had more information regarding them, but the realities of eternity are so far beyond our frame of reference that even the most comprehensive information could not satisfy our desire to know all that eternity holds.

Does that mean that we should forget about eternity and just resign ourselves to the here and now?

GETTING A HANDLE ON HEAVEN

God seems to want us to anticipate eternity, to make decisions in light of eternity and to look forward to embracing eternity. He provides some degree of information in the Bible, mostly metaphors that can help us begin to understand eternity from our limited frame of reference. For example:

> Thus says the LORD: "Heaven is My throne . . ." (Isaiah 66:1*a*).

When we think of a throne, we think of the seat of majesty; that place in which a ruler is present in all of his or her regalia. The throne symbolizes supreme authority. All of Heaven is God's throne. There is no part of Heaven that is not subject to and in agreement with God's will. If you know much about God's character, you know that his will is for people to love one another wholeheartedly and to treat one another with dignity. Even more, his will is also that people should know and enjoy him forever. So Heaven is a place where the rule of these (and many other wonderful things we have yet to comprehend about God's will) are a constant, eternal reality.

Another example that helps us to imagine Heaven is from the New Testament portion of the Bible, in which Jesus assured his followers:

> In My Father's house are many mansions; if it were not so,
> I would have told you. I go to prepare a place for you
> (John 14:2).

All of us can relate to the experience of walking into a friend's home for the first time. We immediately begin to gain a new perspective, a new appreciation of who our friend is, what she likes and what she values. Suddenly, we see aspects of her personality in a new light as we enter her home, the environment she has created according to her taste and pleasure.

Heaven is God's home. It is the place that most reflects his personality, what he likes and what he values. Heaven is where God makes known his presence most fully. It is not a place in the sense that we normally think of, i.e., a site that has spatial boundaries. It is a real place that includes more than that, not less. God created Heaven according to his own taste and pleasure, it is not some amorphous concept.

According to the New Testament, there is a home in Heaven for those who call God their father and who know his son, Jesus. In other words, Heaven is populated by those who want to be where God is. And just as it is not restricted by spatial boundaries, it transcends the boundaries of time. Heaven is a present reality as well as a future hope. It will exist for all eternity, it already exists and those who know God catch glimpses of it. We who have experienced God's presence in a tangible way and have known the joy of being in the middle of his will would find it difficult to explain—but we treasure the experiences. They help us through the hard times because we can look forward to the day when the slices of Heaven we have tasted will become the full measure of our existence forever and ever.

In eternity, Heaven will be the universal reality because God will enlarge his habitation—that is he will expand the place where his presence is made known in all its fullness—to include every person who belongs to him. In fact, the Bible tells us that at that point, God will create a new Heaven and a new Earth. Time and eternity, Heaven and Earth, will join together to most fully reflect the person of God and the place where he lives.

Now I saw a new heaven and a new earth, for the first
heaven and the first earth had passed away. Also there
was no more sea. Then I, John, saw the holy city, New
Jerusalem, coming down out of heaven from God,
prepared as a bride adorned for her husband
(Revelation 21:1,2).

God will dwell with people, will be right in their midst, just
as his presence was manifest in the ark of the covenant so that
he could be with the children of Israel in a tangible way. Only
it will be as if the whole universe is the ark of the covenant,
filled with his glory.

And I heard a loud voice from heaven saying, "Behold,
the tabernacle of God is with men, and He will dwell
with them, and they shall be His people. God Himself will
be with them and be their God (Revelation 21:3).

The Heaven that awaits us in eternity is different from
anything we have ever experienced. We will experience a
whole new level of intimacy with God. It is difficult to know
what that will be like, but this much we do know: there is no
more sorrow, no more death, no more mourning, no more
crying, no more pain, because the very presence of God will
banish all of those agonizing experiences.

THE NEW JERUSALEM: BACK TO THE GARDEN

We have some interesting descriptions of the New
Jerusalem, which seems to be the capital of eternity, from the
Bible's perspective. Some of this may be purely symbolic, but it
gives us a sense of a wonderful new order that God will
establish.

The New Jerusalem is described as a beautiful place of jasper
and gold, yet we are told that it is clear like glass. Neither jasper
nor gold is clear like glass. Jasper is opaque and gold is thick,

yet in the New Jerusalem they will be clear. The foundations all have decorations, each with a different stone. Each of these twelve stones is a different color. The gates resemble huge single pearls. Pearly gates isn't just a saying, it is a description, perhaps symbolic but no less real because of the symbolism. All of this color, precious stone and metal is symbolic of complete purity, incredible beauty and indescribable worth. The magnificent gates are always open. There are no enemies to fear. Access to God is always assured. There will be no Temple in the New Jerusalem. The city itself becomes the sanctuary and the Lord God is its light. Illumined by the glory of the presence of God, there is no more need for the sun or moon. Does that mean there is no sun or moon? I don't know, but the Bible says there is no need for them.

We are also told of a wonderful river, running fast and fresh with the water of life. The tree of life bears fruit on both sides of the river. This imagery takes us back to the Garden of Eden. Originally, God dwelled with the people he created. We were in his presence. There was intimacy with God. But then Adam and Eve chose to rebel against God, to do things their own way. The Lord God expelled them from the garden to deny them access to the tree of life. God knew that it would be Hell on Earth for Adam and Eve to live forever in their sinful state. But what do we see in eternity? Access once again. We are back in the garden, complete with the tree of life. But God's presence, his dwelling with us, is what makes Heaven heaven.

That understanding provides a basis for another understanding: the fact that another place, another destination which is the opposite of Heaven must exist.

A GLIMPSE OF HELL

As much as Heaven is a part of eternity, so is Hell, and we need to wrestle with that reality. Many people today doubt the existence of Hell. Many would like to believe that such a place could not possibly be. Perhaps you've heard about the tombstone with the inscription, "Here lies an atheist, all dressed up and no place to go." That atheist could only wish that were true. Others may laugh off the notion of Hell and glibly say, "I want to go to Hell, because that's where all my friends will be." Unfortunately, the "fellowship" in Hell, if one can call it that, will be comfortless and devoid of meaning.

Hobbes said, "Hell is truth seen too late." All too many people will discover too late that Hell is a place of utter isolation. Instead of a place where they will see all their friends, Hell is the place where no one sees past his or her own misery.

If Heaven is the ultimate joining of God with his people, Hell is his ultimate and final separation from those who are not his. The alienation people experience from God has its outworkings in alienation with one another. Our very ability to relate was created to be satisfied by a relationship with God; other relationships are meant to add to and complement our relationship with him. When there is no longer any possibility of relating to God, our ability to care for others eventually shrivels and dies. That is the nature of the very real place called Hell.

The prophet Daniel clearly saw an eternity that includes a place of judgment as well as bliss:

> And many of those who sleep in the dust of the earth shall awake, some to everlasting life, some to shame and everlasting contempt (Daniel 12:2).

But why? Why would a good and loving God allow human beings to end up in such a place? Hell is primarily about God's ultimate justice. He establishes his justice in a tangible way through the reality of retribution or punishment. Many people view Hell in a purely punitive sense; that God is "getting back" at people for what they have done. But the Bible teaches something different. God will ultimately right all wrongs—and Hell is the right place for people who wrongly do not trust God or want him interfering in their lives.

We look at the evil in the world today and wonder if there is any justice. Well, if Hell does not exist, there is no justice. Hell is the ultimate resolution of the problem of evil. We might wish to see the problem resolved in a "nice" way, but God is good enough and wise enough to resolve it in the only right way. God knows that evil can never be developed into good. Time does not heal it. Look at it this way: a wrong sum can only be put right by going back to the point at which you find the error, and working it again in a correct way. It can never be corrected simply by going on. Part of the nature of evil is a refusal to go back to the point of error. Evil always justifies itself and insists on continuing its own way.

The second accomplishment of Hell is to demonstrate God's holiness. Theologian David Welles says, if God is as good as the Bible says, if his character is as pure, if his life is as infinite, then sin is as infinitely unpardonable and not merely momentarily mischievous. To be commensurate with the offense, God's response must be correspondingly infinite.

C.S. Lewis speaks of the judgment of Hell and the establishment of Heaven as "The Great Divorce." He points out that God must separate holiness from evil, goodness from wickedness. This is in keeping with the Hebrew concept of holiness. The Hebrew word, *Kadosh,* means "holy" or "separate." Lewis says,

> If we insist on keeping hell, we shall not see heaven. If we accept heaven, we shall not be able to retain even the smallest and most intimate souvenirs of hell. Hell is the eternal absence of God, along with the hopelessness of knowing that absence is permanent. The lost enjoy forever the horrible freedom they have demanded, and are therefore, enslaved.

The display of God's holiness and all of his characteristics requires that he remove himself from all that is unholy.

Some don't believe in Hell because they think it represents some form of divine overreaction to a bad deed or choice made along the way. On the contrary, Hell is the real result of a lifetime of wrong choices, as this parable illustrates:

A rich miser once bought a piece of pastry. As he was walking along, he dropped the pastry and when he picked it up, it was covered with dirt. Just then, a beggar came by and asked for charity. The miser handed him the dirty pastry. That night, the miser dreamed he was sitting in a large, crowded cafe. The waiters were running back and forth bringing all the customers the most delicious cakes and tortes. He alone was not being served. He finally complained. Along came a waiter and served him a piece of dirty pastry. "How dare you bring me a piece of dirty pastry?" the rich miser furiously demanded. "Did I ask you for charity? I'm a rich man and there's nothing the matter with my money." "I'm afraid you're mistaken, sir," the waiter replied. "Your money is worthless here. You've just arrived in eternity and all you can order here is what you yourself have sent to heaven from the world of time. The one thing you sent was this piece of pastry and that's all that you can be served with."

Our whole society cries out and says, "You deserve to be happy, whatever it takes," "Take what you want, and give only when you have to or if it makes you feel good." "Have it your way." And God says, "Okay. You can have what you want, you can take what you want; you can have your way instead of my way. You can have your own company instead of my presence. Have it. Have it forever. I'm not going to have you." If sin is man saying to God, "Go away and leave me alone," then Hell is God's way of saying, "Your wish is granted."

Once again, there is the matter of a miscalculated sum. God gives people a chance to go back and discover the error, to come up with the solution he has provided—to find our destiny with him. Yet the opportunity to go back is limited—not because God doesn't want to give us enough of a chance, but because we can become set in unwillingness to ask him to show us our error. Lewis described Hell as a place where the door is locked from the inside.

Milton captured the attitude of Satan: "I would rather reign in

Hell than serve in Heaven." God said, "Okay." Hell is the just reward for sin or error, which in one sense consists of all the choices that fall short of God's standards. But the final error is the refusal to turn back and have it corrected, and that error corresponds to the refusing of God's atonement, the gift of forgiveness and eternal life that he offers through the Messiah Jesus.

Hell is a place of judgment, everlasting or final punishment. It's hard for us to think about the suffering, but that is a reality we cannot afford to dismiss. The Bible is clear that Hell is a conscious torment, that there is weeping and gnashing of teeth there. That phrase, "weeping and gnashing of teeth" is a Hebrew colloquialism. It conveys sorrow and anger coming together. Sorrow at all the possibilities that are lost forever. And anger because there is no acceptance of God's verdict. Hell is a place of condemnation, not only because people are condemned to be there, but because they are full of condemnation, blaming God, blaming others, perhaps even blaming themselves, but without any sense of true repentance.

Whether or not you can bring yourself to believe in the reality of Hell, perhaps reading this helps you understand why believers in Jesus are so passionate about telling others about him. When you believe in the reality of Heaven and Hell, you want to do your best to see that the people you care for are headed for an eternity of joy and not horrific suffering.

HEAVEN OR HELL: THE ULTIMATE CHOICE

We who believe the biblical realities of Heaven and Hell can't help but see the stark choice. Would you choose the absence of all hope and all life and all fellowship with the creator of the universe? Or would you choose that place where God dwells with his people?

Maybe if people had a clearer vision of what God is inviting us to, they would see more significance to the choices made here and now.

What is it really like to be in God's presence? Some actually fear that Heaven will be a boring place with boring people doing boring things. Far from it! King David said, "You will show me the path of life; in Your presence is fullness of joy; at Your right hand are pleasures forevermore" (Psalm 16:11).

The Bible makes a few attempts to describe these pleasures, but the effort leaves us with as many questions as answers. Again, we simply don't have the frame of reference to comprehend the pleasures of Heaven. They will somehow be deeper and more meaningful than any pleasures we have known.

Think about the most incredible view of nature you have seen, the one that filled you with so much wonder that it practically hurt. Or the most moving piece of music you've ever heard, where you just wanted to close your eyes and lose yourself in the rhythm, soar with the melody, unite with the harmony. Think about a piece of art that drew you in and made you yearn to know the person who created it. Reflect on a moment in your life when you were absolutely certain that someone you love, loved you completely and without reservation. If you can relate to even one of those experiences, you have a starting place to imagine a fraction of the pleasure that awaits us in Heaven.

The purest, most exquisite joys that we can experience on this Earth are just a shadow of the glorious eternity that God invites us to share with him. In eternity you will constantly be filled with awe at the wonders that surround you, beauty that will be utterly engrossing.

Those who fear leaving behind the pleasures that we can have in this life don't realize that the delights of Heaven are beyond our imagination because they are more intense, not less so than those we experience now.

For example, some have said, "If there's no sex in Heaven I sure don't want to go." C.S. Lewis explains that offering the pleasures of Heaven in place of earthly pleasures is like telling a child that he won't be able to eat chocolate while having sex. The child can't imagine why would anyone want to give up chocolate for sex. He hasn't yet developed an appetite for sex and therefore can't conceive of the fact that during sex, no one thinks about chocolate. Chocolate is not even an issue.

In the same way, our current longings do not begin to anticipate the delights that we'll be ready for in Heaven. God will fully satisfy our appetite for pleasures we don't yet know how to enjoy. The nature of our relationships will change and we will be fulfilled in ways that are beyond our current frame of reference. The prophet Isaiah wrote: "For behold, I create new heavens and a new earth; and the former shall not be remembered or come to mind" (Isaiah 65:17). He's not talking about some kind of cosmic amnesia, but the fact that God is preparing something so wonderful that we couldn't possibly think of anything better; there will be nothing missing to complete our joy, no past experiences to compete with it.

As American writer and theologian Jonathan Edwards was on his deathbed, his wife was traveling abroad. She did not make it back before his death. He left her a word of hope: "Because our relationship, I believe, is of such a nature as spiritual, it will endure." Jonathan Edwards understood something about Heaven. All that is good and pure and eternal about what we enjoy on this earth will be present, in fact will be enhanced and made more real and wonderful in God's presence, in eternity.

In this world we have a perpetual sense of not fitting, of not finding, of grasping after tiny tastes of joy, small samples of peace, pursuing little snatches of happiness. Those things which seem so fleeting now are the things that God wants us to enjoy in full, in ways we don't yet understand, throughout eternity.

Throughout Scripture, God is calling to us saying, "I want to invite you to real peace. I want to invite you to real joy. I want to invite you to a life with no fear. I want to invite you to a life with no shame. I want to invite you to leave all these things behind and fill yourself with the good things I have provided for you." Ultimately, God will take those of us who belong to him to that place, the place where we do fulfill our ultimate meaning, our purpose, our ultimate joy, our ultimate peace. This is the future hope of the child of God.

Future Hope is a person as well as a place. It is a destination as well as a present reality. God wants you to have that future hope here and now. If you have read this far and have yet to experience the hope, the joy, the peace and forgiveness that God gives, don't wait any longer. Time is fleeting, but God's hope lasts forever. Invite Y'shua to be your great hope and Savior for now and forever. He is waiting.

APPENDIX 1

How to have future hope

If you are ready to believe that God is the source of hope for the future, not only in the arena of world events, but in the area of your personal well-being, please consider the following:

1. God cares about you and wants you to have future hope.

   "'For I know the thoughts that I think toward you,' says the LORD, 'thoughts of peace and not of evil, to give you a future and a hope'" (Jeremiah 29:11).

2. Sin has interfered with the future that God wants to offer you.

   "But your iniquities have separated you from your God, and your sins have hidden His face from you, so that He will not hear" (Isaiah 59:2).

3. God sent Y'shua (Jesus) to be your Sin Bearer and Savior.

   "But He was wounded for our transgressions, He was bruised for our iniquities; the chastisement for our peace was upon Him, and by His stripes we are healed" (Isaiah 53:5).

4. You can receive forgiveness of sins and a forever future with God by accepting what Y'shua did for you, and putting your faith in him.

   "If you confess with your mouth the Lord Y'shua and believe in your heart that God has raised Him from the dead, you will be saved. For with the heart one believes unto righteousness, and with the mouth confession is made unto salvation" (Romans 10:9,10).

If you believe these verses and are ready to begin your future with God right now, this is a prayer that will help you begin a new life:

"Dear God, I know that I have sinned against you and I want to turn from my sin. I believe you provided Y'shua, Jesus, as an atonement for me. With this prayer I receive Jesus as my Savior and my Lord. Thank you God for cleansing me of sin, for healing my soul and for sealing my name in your Book of Life so that I can be with you forever. Please help me to live the life you have for me through Messiah. Amen."

If you just prayed this prayer or if you are considering doing so, please let us hear from you by filling out and returning the coupon on the last page of this book (page 155).

DANIEL'S SEVENTY

SEVENTY WEEKS ARE DETERMINED FOR

From the going forth
of the commandment
to restore and to
build Jerusalem ·······

unto ············ Messiah's death
(April 3, A.D. 33)
and resurrection:
cut off after 69 weeks;
city destroyed A.D. 70

JERUSALEM REBUILT

"SEVEN WEEKS" AND "THREESCORE AND TWO WEEKS"

JERUSALEM DESTROYED

$69 \times 7 \times 360 = 173,880$ days

(March 5, 444 B.C. plus 173,880 days = March 30, A.D. 33)

Nehemiah 2:1-8
20th Year of Artaxerxes
Month of Nisan—First day
March 5, 444 B.C.

March 30, A.D. 33
Luke 19:28-44
Triumphal Entry
Zechariah 9:9

WEEKS

DANIEL 9:24-27

YOUR PEOPLE AND FOR YOUR HOLY CITY

He shall confirm a
covenant with many
for one week
Daniel 9:27

Messiah
returns
with power
Revelation 19:11

PROPHETIC
PARENTHESIS

ONE WEEK

MESSIANIC
KINGDOM

1260
days

42
months

Daniel 9:27

But in the middle of the week
he shall bring an end
to sacrifice

THE DIFFERENCE RAPTURE AND THE

The Bible does not say specifically when the Rapture will occur, which is why there are competing views on the topic. The two most widely held views are that it will occur just prior to the Great Tribulation or just after the Tribulation, at the return of Messiah. Each position involves some degree of speculation.

I personally hold to the first of those opinions, known as the "pre-tribulation" view of the Rapture. According to this view, the Great Tribulation ends, not with the Rapture but with the Revelation of Messiah. In other words, at the Rapture, Jesus removes from the earth all who believe in him before the Great Tribulation. His return at the end is what is known as the "Second Coming." This chart distinguishes between the two.

The event:

Who is involved:

What happens:

Where it happens:

When it happens:

Why it happens:

How it happens:

BETWEEN THE SECOND COMING

Rapture of the believers	Return of Messiah
Only the believers in Jesus	All humanity
Believers "caught away"	Messiah appears
In the air	On the Earth (Mount of Olives)
Before wrath	After wrath
Save believers from wrath	Save Israel from the Antichrist
Surprise— like a thief in the night	Climax of clearly unfolding events

APPENDIX 4

Is the Antichrist Jewish?

Some have speculated that the Antichrist is or will be Jewish. Following are five good reasons to believe that the Antichrist is not Jewish:

1. Some base their belief that the Antichrist is Jewish on the verse in Daniel that says, "He will have no regard for the God of his fathers." However the Hebrew is actually more properly translated, "the gods of his fathers" and therefore, it would seem to indicate the very opposite, since the Jewish people have but one God.

2. When Daniel prophesies about the Antichrist, he compares him to other kings (Daniel 7,8,11). These kings are pictured as horns, and the Antichrist is depicted as the final and most powerful of them all. In this section of Daniel, horns (a symbol of strength) are used to describe the Gentile nations, never Israel. And since none of the kings (or horns) Daniel previously describes are Jewish, it seems unlikely that the most powerful of them would be Jewish either.

3. Revelation 13 depicts the Antichrist as "rising out of the sea." In the Bible, "the land" is often seen as a metaphor for the nation of Israel and the Jewish people while "the sea" is a metaphor for the (non-Jewish) nations of the earth.

4. Antiochus is a central figure in Daniel's prophecy. He is the precursor, the type of the Antichrist. Antiochus was Syrian, not Jewish. Again, this lends to a non-Jewish Antichrist position.

5. Daniel 9:27 describes the Antichrist as, "the prince of the people who will come and destroy the city." The people who came and destroyed the city of Jerusalem in A.D. 70 were the Romans—definitely not Jews. Some may say, as a result, that the Antichrist is actually from Italy or Romania. Whether he is Italian, Romanian or Syrian is not at all clear. It does seem clear, however, that he is not Jewish.

ISRAEL'S FOUR

Messiah's
First
Coming

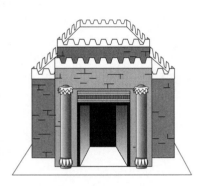

First Temple
(Solomon's)

(1 Kings 5-8)

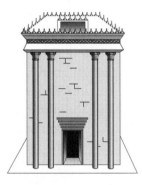

Second Temple
(Zerubbabel's & Herod's)

(Ezra 3:7-6:18)

374 Years	70 Years	586 Years		
960 B.C.	588 B.C.	515 B.C.	20 B.C.	A.D. 70
First	First	Second	Second	Second
Temple	Temple	Temple	Temple	Temple
Built	Destroyed	Built	Enlarged	Destroyed

TEMPLES

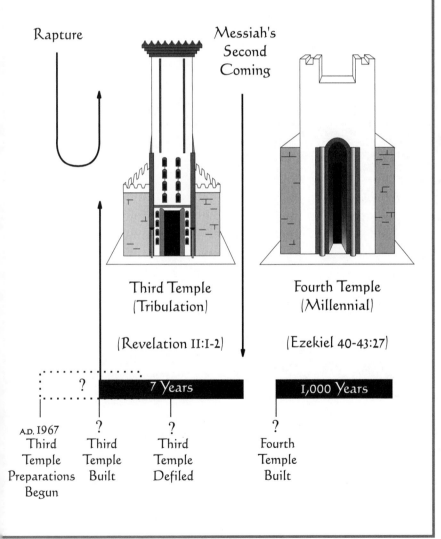

Rapture

Messiah's
Second
Coming

Third Temple
(Tribulation)

(Revelation 11:1-2)

Fourth Temple
(Millennial)

(Ezekiel 40-43:27)

?   7 Years   1,000 Years

A.D. 1967
Third
Temple
Preparations
Begun

?
Third
Temple
Built

?
Third
Temple
Defiled

?
Fourth
Temple
Built

TRIBULATION

7 SEALS
Revelation 6:1-17

7 TRUMPETS
Revelation 8:1-9:21

JUDGMENTS

7 BOWLS
Revelation 16:1-21

THE THRONE

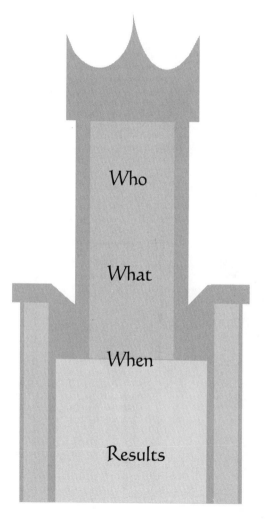

Judgment Seat
of Messiah
(2 Corintians 5:10)

Who — Believers
in Jesus

What — Works done
during lifetime

When — At the Rapture

Results — Rewards
given

JUDGMENTS

Judgment of the Nations (Joel 3:12-16)	Judgment of the Great White Throne (Revelation 20:11f)
All people who followed the Antichrist & False Prophet; Nations opposing Israel	All the dead; all living at the end of Millennium; Satan, death and Hades
Whose side they chose	Whose name is written in the Book of Life
At the Return of Messiah	At the end of the Millennium
Establish the Millennial Kingdom	Usher in eternity

APPENDIX 8

Hastening Messiah's Return

Can we hasten the coming of the Messiah to Earth by our own actions? Certainly some ultra-Orthodox Jewish teaching leans that way. Some rabbis teach that if all the Jews of the world observe one Sabbath the Messiah will appear.

In an ironic twist, some people within the Jewish community have been warning that Christians will step up their "proselytizing" of Jewish people in light of the turn of the millennium. They are creating the impression that Christians think Jews are preventing the coming of Jesus by not believing in him. They say that Christians want Jews to believe in Jesus in order to hasten his return, and have even hinted that Christians who expect Jesus to return in the year 2000 will be disappointed and angry with the Jewish people when he does not.

It is not part of the Christian belief that Jesus will return in the year 2000, nor is it part of the Christian belief that Jewish people must believe in him before he can return. The fact that Jewish people are being told such things creates an unnecessary wedge of fear and suspicion.

If there are Christians who believe that people can hasten the return of Messiah by their actions or beliefs, they are a decided minority and sorely misinformed. Those who believe the Bible know that on such matters God is sovereign. In other words, he is calling the shots and we are not in any position to either move him along any faster or delay his hand concerning the Messiah's return. To think otherwise is to make the same mistake that our matriarch, Sarah made.

God promised Abraham an heir through Sarah, but she didn't believe it could happen—or perhaps she felt God was taking altogether too much time. So she offered her maidservant, Hagar to her husband, so that he could father a child through her. As a result, Ishmael was born. Later, God fulfilled his promise and Sarah gave birth to Isaac, but there has been pain and conflict between the descendants of Isaac and Ishmael ever since.

God doesn't need our help to accomplish his plans. His timing is perfect and it rarely coincides with our wishes. Most Christians who urgently share their faith with Jews or Gentiles, do so out of a strong conviction that God wants them to. They are also compelled by care and concern because they truly believe that following Jesus is the path to joy, peace and forgiveness—and that a choice for him is the greatest choice that any human being could make.

THE SITES OF THE END TIMES

Jerusalem and the Kidron Valley (Valley of Jehoshaphat). The site of the final battle and judgment of the nations. *(Photo by Paige Saunders.)*

Mount of Olives: The place of Messiah's return. *(Photo from Davka Graphics.)*

The Temple Mount, Jerusalem. The site for the Third Temple, the Abomination of Desolation. *(Photo by Susan Perlman.)*

Megiddo (Armageddon): The gathering place for the final conflict. *(Photo by Susan Perlman.)*

BIBLIOGRAPHY

Blackstone, William E. *Jesus is Coming.* Old Tappan, N.J.: Revell, 1932.

Epstein, I., ed. *The Babylonian Talmud.* London: Soncino, 1935.

Erickson, Millard J. *Christian Theology.* Grand Rapids: Baker, 1985.

Fruchtenbaum, Arnold G. *The Footsteps of the Messiah.* Tustin: Ariel Ministries, 1983.

Goldberg, Louis. *Turbulence Over the Middle East.* Neptune, N.J.: Loizeaux Brothers, 1982.

Hoehner, Harold W. *Chronological Aspects of the Life of Christ.* Grand Rapids: Zondervan, 1977.

Hoyt, Herman A. *The End Times.* Chicago: Moody, 1969.

Jeremiah, David with C.C. Carlson. *Escape the Coming Night.* Dallas: Word, 1997.

Larsen, David L. *Jews, Gentiles and the Church.* Grand Rapids: Discovery House, 1995.

Lewis, C.S. *The Great Divorce.* New York: Macmillan, 1946.

Lewis, C.S. *Mere Christianity.* New York: Collier, 1960.

Lewis, C.S. *The Problem of Pain.* New York: Macmillan, 1962.

McClain, Alva J. *Daniel's Prophecy of the 70 Weeks.* Grand Rapids: Zondervan, 1969.

Montefiore, C.G. and H. Loewe. *A Rabbinic Anthology.* New York: Schocken, 1974.

Pache, René. *The Future Life.* Chicago: Moody, 1962.

Patai, Raphael. *The Messiah Texts.* New York: Avon, 1979.

Pentecost, J. Dwight. *Things to Come: A Study in Biblical Eschatology.* Grand Rapids: Dunham, 1958.

VanKampen, Robert. *The Sign.* Wheaton: Crossway, 1992.

RECOMMENDED READING LIST

Cohen, Steve. *Disowned!* San Francisco: Purple Pomegranate, 1995.

Dorsett, Lyle W. *And God Came In.* New York: Good News Publishers, 1983.

Frydland, Rachmiel. *When Being Jewish Was a Crime.* Nashville: Thomas Nelson, 1978.

Harvey, Richard. *But I'm Jewish.* San Francisco: Purple Pomegranate, 1996.

Jews for Jesus Staff. *The Y'shua Challenge, Part I.* San Francisco: Purple Pomegranate, 1993.

Leman, Derek. *The Y'shua Challenge, Part II: A Basic Study Guide.* San Francisco: Purple Pomegranate, 1998.

Lewis, C.S. *Mere Christianity.* New York: Collier Macmillan, 1960.

Lewis, C.S. *Miracles.* New York: Macmillan, 1978.

Lewis, C.S. *The Problem of Pain.* New York: Macmillan, 1978.

McDowell, Josh. *Evidence That Demands a Verdict: Historical Evidences for the Christian Faith.* San Bernardino, CA: Campus Crusade for Christ International, 1972.

McDowell, Josh. *More Than a Carpenter.* Wheaton: Tyndale, 1977.

McDowell, Josh and Don Stewart. *Answers to Tough Questions.* Nashville: Thomas Nelson, 1980.

Questions and Answers. San Francisco: Purple Pomegranate, 1983.

Rosen, Moishe. *The Universe is Broken—Who on Earth Can Fix It?* San Francisco: Purple Pomegranate, 1991.

Rosen, Moishe. *Y'shua.* Chicago: Moody Press, 1982.

Rosen, Ruth, ed. *Jewish Doctors Meet the Great Physician.* San Francisco: Purple Pomegranate, 1998.

Rosen, Ruth, ed. *Testimonies.* San Francisco: Purple Pomegranate, 1992.

Roth, Sid with Irene Harrell. *There Must Be Something More!* Brunswick, GA: Messianic Vision, 1994.

Stern, David H., trans. *Jewish New Testament.* Clarksville, MD: Jewish New Testament Publications, 1992.

Telchin, Stan. *Betrayed.* Grand Rapids: Baker, 1981.

Ten Boom, Corrie and John Sherrill. *The Hiding Place.* New York: Bantam Books, 1984.

All books listed above are available through Purple Pomegranate Productions, 80 Page Street, San Francisco, CA 94102-5914. (415) 864-3900, E-mail: Purplepome@aol.com

If you just prayed the prayer on page 130 or if you are considering doing so, please let us hear from you by filling out and returning this coupon:

(Please print)

Name _____

Street _____

City _____ State _____ Zip _____

Phone (___)_____

E-mail _____

❑ I read the texts from the Bible and prayed the prayer. I sign my name as a commitment to Y'shua as my Savior and Lord.

Signed _____

Date _____

❑ I really don't understand or believe these texts yet but I am seriously willing to consider them and seek what God has for me.

❑ I already believe in Y'shua and want to know more about Jews for Jesus.

I am ❑ Jewish ❑ Gentile

Please return to:
Jews for Jesus/Future Hope
60 Haight Street
San Francisco, CA 94102-5895
E-mail: jfj@jewsforjesus.org
www.jewsforjesus.org

WMDECFH